Other books by the author

Beyond Survival: Emerging Dimensions of Indian Economy (1984)
Off the Track (1987)
Saga of Struggle and Sacrifice (1992)
Challenges Before the Nation (1992)
Thoughts and Reflections (2014)
The Dramatic Decade: The Indira Gandhi Years (2014)
The Turbulent Years (2016)
The Coalition Years (2017)

THE PRESIDENTIAL YEARS 2012–2017

PRANAB MUKHERJEE

Published by
Rupa Publications India Pvt. Ltd 2021
7/16, Ansari Road, Daryaganj
New Delhi 110002

Sales Centres:

Allahabad Bengaluru Chennai
Hyderabad Jaipur Kathmandu
Kolkata Mumbai

Copyright © Pranab Mukherjee 2021

Photos copyright: RB-Photo

The views and opinions expressed in this book are the author's own and the facts are as reported by him which have been verified to the extent possible, and the publishers are not in any way liable for the same.

All rights reserved.

No part of this publication may be reproduced, transmitted, or stored in a retrieval system, in any form or by any means, electronic, mechanical, photocopying, recording or otherwise, without the prior permission of the publisher.

ISBN: 978-93-90356-35-5

Third impression 2021

10 9 8 7 6 5 4 3

The moral right of the author has been asserted.

Printed at Parksons Graphics Pvt. Ltd, Mumbai

This book is sold subject to the condition that it shall not, by way of trade or otherwise, be lent, resold, hired out, or otherwise circulated, without the publisher's prior consent, in any form of binding or cover other than that in which it is published.

*Dedicated to
India's democracy,
which was responsible for a journey that brought me
from the flicker of a lamp in a remote village in Bengal
to the chandeliers of Rashtrapati Bhavan*

CONTENTS

Introduction ix

1. Reflections on Parliament: Value of Dissent and Power 1
2. Elections 2014: Not a Turning Point, but Historic 15
3. Of Presidential Addresses: Both Candid and Cautious 25
4. Article 356 and India's Federal Spirit: Use and Misuse 44
5. Judiciary, the Pillar of Democracy: Its Reach; Its Limits 61
6. Dealing with Mercy Petitions: Humane and Legal Aspects 72
7. Foreign Policy: Maintaining Balance; Using Leverage 83
8. Presidential Visits Abroad: Reiterating Friendship and Cooperation 114
9. Interacting with Leaders: Of Heads of State and Government 143

10. Path-breaking Decisions:
    Story of Demonetization and GST   155

11. My Prime Ministers:
    Different Styles, Different Temperaments   167

Epilogue   177

Index   183

INTRODUCTION

The year was 2012. Monsoon had reached India, caressing most parts of the country. The southern and western parts of the country were, of course, awash with it. But on that day—25 July—neither the clouds nor the rain had deigned to cast their benevolent glance on Delhi. It was hot and sultry. I remember it vividly because it was a momentous moment for me. It was on this day that I took oath as the 13th President of the Republic of India. And, while I was fully dressed for the occasion, in a black achkan and white churidar, it wasn't what I would have wished to wear on an ordinary humid day.

The ceremony began with the arrival from Rashtrapati Bhavan of the outgoing President Pratibha Devisingh Patil and me at the Parliament House, where I was greeted warmly by Vice President Hamid Ansari, and Chief Justice of India (CJI) S.H. Kapadia. I was then escorted to the Central Hall, which has witnessed many watershed moments in the country's political history. It was here that the Constituent Assembly had met for years to discuss and deliberate on the future of free India. It was here that the Constitution of India was debated and adopted by stalwarts, all of them iconic figures, who were members of the Constituent Assembly. And it is in the Central Hall that joint sessions of Parliament are held and where the president addresses both the Houses, usually during the first sitting of Parliament in the year, or the first sitting of Parliament after a new government takes over at the Centre.

The air-conditioning at the packed-to-capacity Central Hall of Parliament and the slow whirring of fans in addition, offered the much-needed relief from the sultry weather. A large gathering of dignitaries, including Prime Minister (PM) Dr Manmohan Singh, Lok Sabha Speaker Meira Kumar, United Progressive Alliance (UPA) Chairperson Sonia Gandhi, union ministers, governors and prominent opposition party leaders, was in attendance to witness the ceremony, as I stood to take oath, administered by the CJI. It was a short one, as per tradition:

> I, Pranab Mukherjee, do swear in the name of God that I will faithfully execute the office of President of the Republic of India, and will to the best of my ability preserve, protect and defend the Constitution and the law, and that I will devote myself to the service and well-being of the people of the Republic of India.

I felt goosebumps as I read the lines that administered me the oath. I would now be following in the footsteps of my illustrious predecessors such as Dr Rajendra Prasad, Dr S. Radhakrishnan, Dr Zakir Husain and Dr A.P.J. Abdul Kalam, among others. I had to live up to both the dignity of the office I was assuming and the legacy of the stellar work that the other occupants of Rashtrapati Bhavan had left behind.

The ceremony was marked by pomp and grandeur. It was something to which I was no stranger, having been part of gatherings on a few occasions previously when presidents took the oath of office. Nonetheless, the experience of being at the centre stage of the event was unique and left me overwhelmed. A 21-gun salute announced the swearing-in of the new president. This was followed by a thunderous applause and thumping of desks from the dignitaries when I signed the oath register.

Once the formalities inside the Parliament building were over, my immediate predecessor and I were led out of the Central Hall amid the roll of drums and the blowing of trumpets. The outgoing president and her husband, Dr Devisingh Ransingh Shekhawat, were among the many who congratulated me and wished me well in my new assignment.

Back at Rashtrapati Bhavan, I inspected a tri-services guard of honour and then escorted Pratibha Patil to her residence at 2, Tughlaq Lane.

The ceremony done, I walked into my study in the sprawling and magnificent Rashtrapati Bhavan. Like the Central Hall, Rashtrapati Bhavan too is steeped in history, made deeper by the illustrious occupants of the past. It was not the first time that I was visiting the grand residence; I had been there on various occasions in connection with a number of official engagements and missions for my erstwhile party, the Congress, and on social occasions hosted by the president of the day. But again, given the fact that I was now the occupant of Rashtrapati Bhavan as the head of state and would be the host on numerous occasions in the coming years, the feeling was very different from that of the past. From the hurly-burly of an extremely busy life of an active politician to the 'life of leisure' as many termed it, I wondered how I would adapt to the challenges that lurked round the corner, and how I would meet them. Of course, it was still too early to lose sleep over those thoughts, and yet the legacies that surrounded the magnificent building could not be forgotten. I just could not afford to fail to live up to those expectations.

From where I stood behind my desk, the view from the window of the study, as the President's office is called, was that of the magnificent Mughal Gardens, often regarded as the 'soul of the Presidential Palace'. The main garden is divided into a grid of squares by two channels running north to south, and two more running from west to east. Lotus-shaped fountains that throw up water to a height of 12 feet, adorn the crossings of these channels. There are two huge lawns, one square and the other oblong. Lush green grass covers the lawns and it takes a great deal of effort and expertise, as I was to learn, to maintain the green carpet. Various trees, common and exotic, make up the gardens, as do a large variety of flowers including tulips and over a hundred varieties of roses. It is a place I soon fell in love with and spent as much time as I could, taking leisurely walks or while contemplating important matters of the state. I am happy that people have an opportunity to visit it when the garden opens up for the public once a year in winters when the flowers are in full bloom.

But the garden was not the only feature to overwhelm me. I noted the expansiveness of Rashtrapati Bhavan with awe. Located at one end of the famous Rajpath in New Delhi, it was constructed as the British Viceroy's residence-cum-office, and was called the Viceroy's House. The first Indian to officially

THE PRESIDENTIAL YEARS

occupy what came to be known as Rashtrapati Bhavan was C. Rajagopalachari, as the Governor General of India. He, however, occupied only a few of the 340-odd rooms that comprise the main Bhavan. The entire Presidential Estate, which includes Rashtrapati Bhavan, is spread over a mind-boggling 320 acres. In terms of area, it is the largest residence of any head of state in the world.

Fascinating as these details were—many of which I had known earlier but only now had the occasion to experience as an official occupant—my thoughts primarily hovered elsewhere. Even as I absorbed the grandeur of my new residence and its interesting history, I mused over where I had reached. Less than two months ago, I had been an active politician, part of the country's oldest political party that had played a defining role in the freedom struggle and boasted of icons like Jawaharlal Nehru and Sardar Patel, and so many more—not to forget Mahatma Gandhi. As a minister in several governments, from those led by Indira Gandhi to Manmohan Singh, I had the occasion to participate in several decisions that had defining consequences for the country and its polity.

I was fortunate to have worked closely with tall leaders like Mrs Gandhi who valued my judgement, and assumed important ministerial responsibilities, including defence, finance, external affairs and commerce in various governments. I had been leader of the Lok Sabha, deputy chairman of the Planning Commission, and a member of both Houses of Parliament at different points in time, for decades. It was a matter of immense satisfaction and pride that I received a great deal of respect and regard from not just my party, but also leaders from opposition parties during my long tenure in active politics.

But those days were now firmly behind me. Although steeped in the Congress's ideology, I was now an apolitical person as president of the country—and supreme commander of the armed forces. It did cross my mind that I had perhaps prematurely bid goodbye to politics when I accepted the offer to be the ruling Congress-led UPA's presidential nominee; my election was a foregone conclusion given the broad support I enjoyed. I felt I still had some more years to give to active politics. However, I quickly banished those thoughts as pointless musings. I was now the president of this great sovereign, socialist, secular, democratic republic of India, and had to think and act accordingly. I had before me the examples of others who had been important members of a political party, who had gone on to become heads of state and distinguished themselves with their non-partisan conduct. There were, of course, a few, who came from outside the political spectrum; space scientist Dr Kalam being one of them.

But whatever may have been their backgrounds, as president, they endeavoured to bring dignity and respect to the high office they held. I was determined to be no different. Therefore, right from the beginning I made it clear that I was finally done with my political role. I had internalized every single word I had spoken while taking oath of office and intended to honour each of those words. As I look back, I can say with a degree of satisfaction that I succeeded in keeping that resolve.

This book is an attempt on my part to place before the readers the functions and duties, and the challenges that I encountered, during my tenure as president. I also seek to explain the ways in which I handled tricky situations. I narrate that, while keeping a distance from politics I was able to win over the trust of political leaders from a spectrum of differing ideologies, guiding them whenever such assistance was required, so long as it did not compromise on my conduct as the head of the state. In a parliamentary form of democracy, such as that in India, the president is considered a titular head, with real power lying with a popularly elected government led by the PM. However, the president has a key role to perform when there is a breakdown in the constitutional scheme of things, or when there are hurdles in the formation of governments in the absence of a clear-cut majority for a party or a combination of parties.

Even otherwise, in normal situations, the president plays a significant role in various matters, such as the improvement of bilateral relations with other countries. A presidential visit on foreign soil is viewed with importance by the host nation. I can say with a level of confidence that I contributed to the improvement in India's ties with countries I visited as president and during which I had interactions with important personalities, including heads of state. In this book, I have given an account of these visits and their outcome.

The functions that the President of India performs are varied, from ceremonial to substantial. I would like to believe that I added substance to many of those functions during my stay at Rashtrapati Bhavan, and I have given an account of a few of these in the following chapters. They include some of the initiatives I took during my interactions with foreign dignitaries, often using the goodwill I enjoyed with them—Bangladesh's Prime Minister Sheikh Hasina is a good example of the latter—for the betterment of relations between India and her neighbours.

Readers will note that I have been somewhat biased to the subject of Bangladesh, which I have dealt with in detail. This is because of both personal and bilateral reasons. I have shared a level of closeness to the family of Sheikh Hasina from the time she was in exile, and have had the occasion to understand the politics of her country from close quarters. I must admit this understanding helped me, both as president and earlier as a functionary of the Congress party and minister, to deepen and expand India–Bangladesh bilateral ties. I am a strong votary of the idea of India developing close ties with her neighbours, and as president, I made it a point to visit our neighbours as often as I could, without, of course, ignoring other key global players.

As president of a democratic country, it was also my duty to ensure that democratic values were respected in all spheres of life, more so in the political arena. I used occasions to speak my mind on contentious matters that troubled society and right-thinking people. I flagged matters of concern, often making my views known without ambiguity and with a certain degree of bluntness. But while I was sensitive to popular sentiments, I was extremely careful, as president, not to be swayed by populism, but to adhere to the exacting standards a president had to meet in such circumstances.

My initial years at Rashtrapati Bhavan saw anger growing against the Dr Manmohan Singh government. I have referred to this phenomenon and tried to explain the causes for it. I have also written about the landslide victory of the Bharatiya Janata Party (BJP) under Narendra Modi's leadership in 2014, but have also highlighted its failures in certain areas during its first term in office and suggested corrective measures.

As president, I had the opportunity to work with two PMs, both very different to each other in style, substance and approach. I have explained my understanding of Narendra Modi and Dr Singh, both as individuals and as PMs. I do not believe in being unduly judgmental, but certain aspects should be spoken about in the larger interests of the country and I have sought to do so in the course of framing my thoughts in the book.

I have always held strong views on the functioning of the judiciary and its interplay with the executive and Parliament. In this book too, I have been candid on the subject. While maintaining that the judiciary, especially higher judiciary, remains a robust institution trusted by millions of Indians for whom the courts are the last refuge to get justice, I have pointed out the transgressions that were sometimes made by the courts in matters of Parliament and the executive. I believe that the judiciary must respect the fine line that divides its jurisdiction from those of the government and Parliament. There have been instances when that has not happened. I believe—and I have given reasons—that the Supreme Court erred in scrapping an act passed by Parliament, which had proposed the creation of a mechanism for the appointment of judges to higher courts.

My views on contentious matters such as demonetization and the introduction of the Goods and Services Tax (GST), both of which happened during my presidentship, have also been mentioned at some length. I have spoken of the opportunity I got in addressing a joint session of Parliament summoned to mark the introduction of GST. I have held the view that GST has happened for the good, while the stated objectives of demonetization were not achieved.

The core purpose of the book is to present before the readers my attempt as president to promote, preserve and propagate the hallowed ideals on which this country rests. Our freedom fighters and framers of the Constitution of India—perhaps among the best articulated and fair documents the world—have toiled hard for decades to give us an India that is free and democratic, and where unity in diversity is our calling card. It is our duty, as citizens, to honour this grand legacy.

CHAPTER 1

REFLECTIONS ON PARLIAMENT: VALUE OF DISSENT AND POWER

Few matters disturb me as much as the culture of meaningless disruptions in Parliament and state assemblies. Having spent decades in public life as a representative of the people, and having had the privilege to serve this great country as its president, I am appalled at the callousness with which disruptions have been used as a tool to hold a government accountable. In a parliamentary democracy, the foremost responsibility of every elected representative in Parliament and state assemblies is to legislate for the greater good of society and the country. Every representative of the people must bear in mind that he or she owes their membership of Parliament or assemblies to the people, as each of the members, and for that matter even the President of India, has to seek votes to get elected.

Ever since I started my parliamentary journey, I would be mesmerized listening to stalwarts in Parliament for hours and days, regardless of whether I was seated in the Treasury or

Opposition benches. This practice helped me unite with the soul of this living institution and understand and appreciate the true value of debate, discussion and dissent. Some of the most outstanding examples of healthy debates are found in the proceedings of the Constituent Assembly of India between 9 December 1946 (when the Constituent Assembly first met) and 26 January 1950 (after which it ceased to exist and was replaced by the Provisional Parliament of India). The Constituent Assembly had met to finalize the Constitution of India, article by article and clause by clause. Nearly every provision was discussed and debated threadbare, with several members raising objections vehemently, and seeking and receiving responses. It was out of this massive churning of ideas and opinions that the Constitution was given shape and adopted. The stalwarts who participated in these discussions belonged to a range of political affiliations and clashed with one another in the course of discussions, and yet all of them worked tirelessly towards the common goal of giving the country a Constitution that would deal with all sections of people without prejudice or undue favour. Dissent did not lead to disruption or deadlock; instead, it facilitated the creation of the best possible Constitution.

In the years that followed, especially during Nehru's prime ministership, the practice of debate, discussion and dissent flourished. Nehru not only encouraged conflict of opinion but also respected it. Several opposition party leaders, including Atal Bihari Vajpayee, made a mark in the House because they were given the opportunity to freely express their thoughts and criticisms of the government of the day. Unfortunately, as time passed by, much of that democratic spirit was replaced by raucous interruptions in the name of discussion and the Opposition's opinions were dealt with contempt.

A SYSTEM OF INSTITUTIONALIZED DISRUPTIONS

When we began our parliamentary democracy, particularly from the first Lok Sabha/Rajya Sabha in 1952, every parliamentary session comprised 12 weeks of the Budget Session and six weeks each of the Monsoon Session and the Winter Session. These were the three normal sessions of Parliament in a year. In more recent years, particularly over the last decade, a totally unacceptable culture of disruptions has harmed this tried and tested system. Meaningless disruptions on flimsy grounds have rendered the Parliament, a fundamental pillar of Indian democracy, ineffective. More dangerously, they have undermined democracy. These can hardly be considered effective parliamentary interventions, and are indeed the ultimate betrayal of commitment to the people of India. It is only through Parliament and legislative assemblies that governments are held accountable to the people. If these institutions themselves become dysfunctional, it not only results in institutional paralysis but also has a ripple effect across the system.

There was a time when the House listened with rapt attention to the stalwarts of the House, whether in the Lok Sabha or the Rajya Sabha. There was constructive criticism as well as informed suggestions from the Opposition benches, and the government of the day took the inputs seriously. But then came the trend when even Budget speeches were interrupted; not even the PM was spared of disruptions when he spoke. This was seen especially during the second term of the UPA government.

I have expressed concern on several occasions regarding the drop in the number of days Parliament transacts business. In the 1950s and 60s, the average number of sittings was 127 days for the Lok Sabha and 93 days for the Rajya Sabha. This is in sharp contrast to 2018, when the second leg of the Budget Session, which started on 5 March and ended on 6 April, saw virtually no business being transacted. This meant that not a single demand of any ministry was considered on the floor of the House.

Of course, in the earlier days, there were no department-related standing committees. The constitution of these standing committees is definitely a sound parliamentary initiative for scrutinizing bills moved by the government on subjects related to the departmental panels. The panels also conduct a brief examination of the Demand for Grants connected with the department after the presentation of the Budget and make suggestions to the House, without altering the demands or recommending any change in the Budget proposed. The standing committee can recommend but cannot suggest changes in the figures, as the power to alter the allocation lies with the full House and not with a part (committee) of it. The views of the committee can be examined or considered by the Ministry of Finance in making proposals for the future.

Despite the important role played by these parliamentary standing committees, their work cannot substitute that of the open session of Parliament. Debates and discussions on the floor of the House have their own impact and there is absolutely no excuse for not holding sessions over a period of time.

Constant disruption of proceedings can also be attributed to the fractured verdicts of the people in 25 years, from 1989 to 2014. The turbulent decade of 1989–99, which should have seen only three general elections (1989, 1994 and 1999) under normal circumstances, was witness to five elections (1989, 1991, 1996, 1998 and 1999). Further, during this decade, Parliament, with a full tenure of five years, came into existence only once—in 1991, under the leadership of P.V. Narasimha Rao. The earlier government in 1989–91 was short-lived, just like the governments that came to power in 1996–98 and 1998–99. Normalcy returned once again from 1999 onwards.

WHEN THE OPPOSITION LOSES MORAL AUTHORITY

I have consistently maintained that disruption hurts the Opposition more than the government, as a disruptive Opposition loses the moral authority to put the government on the mat. It also gives the executive an undue advantage to curtail Parliament sessions on the pretext of the prevailing chaos. On several occasions when I was approached as the leader of the House for extending sessions, I asked if the need for such extension was only to transact some more *halla* (chaotic) business. This agenda of disruptions is not a new phenomenon; in fact, the systematic way in which an entire session, or a substantial part of it, gets disrupted and washed out began in 2004 when the Congress-led UPA assumed power and the BJP-led National Democratic Alliance (NDA) was the main opposition.

There were some indications of this disruptive agenda when the Congress was in opposition during the 13th Lok Sabha, from

1999 to 2004. During this period, the party was responsible for disruptions in the House on several occasions. This resulted in differences between members of the Rajya Sabha and the Lok Sabha. As a member of the Upper House, I, along with Dr Manmohan Singh, opposed the tendency of the party's leadership to support disruptions in the Lower House. I made it amply clear that this practice of disruptions may have become the norm in the Lok Sabha, but it would not be implemented under my leadership in the Rajya Sabha. Dr Singh agreed with me. I further reiterated to the party leadership that it would be better off finding a replacement for me in case it wished to carry forward such tactics. Owing to my stand, we were faced with the happy situation where it was business as usual in the Rajya Sabha, even as the Lower House remained disturbed.

I have always maintained that in Parliament, occasions do get created sometimes when tempers rise and tensions between the ruling and opposition groups get intense. The situation can be defused by cool-headed discussions amongst leaders of the major political parties to adopt a compromise formula on the contentious issues. In such exceptional cases, normalcy has been restored through a process of give and take. I recollect that the Monsoon Session in August 1978 was disrupted when official letters exchanged between the then PM Morarji Desai and former Home Minister Charan Singh appeared in a leading publication. The Members of Parliament (MPs) were vociferous in their demand that, since secret government correspondence had been made public, the letters be placed on the table of the House. It was a tricky situation, which eventually led to a middle path, where the government adopted a resolution to discuss the issue through a substantive motion.

Accordingly, a substantive motion under Rule 170 of Rajya Sabha was moved by N.K.P. Salve on 10 August 1978, urging the government to set up an inquiry commission under a retired judge to look into the allegations and counter-allegations made by the PM and the home minister against each other in the letters exchanged between them. A debate ensued throughout the whole day, and finally the motion was adopted by a majority of members with an amendment. However, nothing really happened after the motion was adopted. Since as per law, the setting up of a commission under the Commission of Inquiry Act 1952 was to be done by the Lok Sabha or Legislative Assembly, not by the Rajya Sabha or Legislative Council. In other words, the Rajya Sabha had no authority of recommending the setting up of a commission of inquiry as per the law prevailing at that point of time.

Though the Opposition did not get anything substantive, through this mechanism, the tension created in the House due to frequent disruptions was resolved and Parliament started functioning normally. My suggestion is that in each case, however sensitive it may be, a solution could be found by having discussions among the leaders.

QUESTION HOUR: VICTIM OF DISRUPTION

Yet another important facet of disruption is its detrimental impact on the Question Hour. Our parliamentary history is peppered with inspiring stories of the manner in which Indians snatched this right from their unwilling colonial masters. The

Indian Councils Act of 1892 saw an appreciable increase in the powers of the legislatures and gave members of the councils the right to ask questions on domestic matters for the first time. At that time, most of the members were nominated. A minuscule percentage was elected by a small electoral college, like members of municipalities, district boards, local boards, university graduates, registered trade unions, trading bodies, etc. When questions were allowed, members like Sir Pherozeshah Mehta, Rash Behari Ghosh, C.R. Das, V.S. Srinivasa Sastri and S. Satyamurti used this opportunity to fully corner the government. The Indian members posed difficult questions to members of the British Executive (who discharged the functions of a minister). Mahatma Gandhi once observed that, if there were 10 Satyamurthys in our council, the British would have left this country long ago. In fact, Mehta's aggression earned him the nickname 'Ferocious Mehta'.

NO PLACE FOR ABSENTEE LEADERSHIP

During the UPA years, I would resolve difficult issues by remaining in constant touch with the leader of the Opposition and senior leaders of both the UPA and the NDA. My job was to run the House, even if it meant meeting and convincing members of the Opposition alliance. I would be present at all times in the House in order to defuse contentious issues, whenever they arose.

Sadly, the Narendra Modi-led NDA government, during its first term of 2014–19, failed in its primary responsibility to ensure the smooth and proper functioning of Parliament. I attribute the acrimonious exchanges between the Treasury and Opposition benches to the arrogance and inept handling by the government. But the Opposition is not without blame either. It had also behaved irresponsibly.

The mere physical presence of the PM in Parliament makes a tremendous difference to the functioning of this institution. Whether it was Jawaharlal Nehru, Indira Gandhi, Atal Bihari Vajpayee or Dr Singh, each of these former PMs made their presence felt on the floor of the House. PM Modi, now in his second term, must take inspiration from his predecessors and provide visible leadership, through his enhanced presence in Parliament to avoid situations that had precipitated the parliamentary crisis we witnessed in the first term. He must listen to the dissenting voices and speak more often in Parliament. He must use it as a forum to disseminate his views to convince the Opposition and inform the nation. As a minister in the Manmohan Singh cabinet, I had sought to defuse the crisis the government faced in the backdrop of the massive agitation that social activist Anna Hazare had led for the institution of the Lokpal. I had suggested that the government consider his three keys demands on the Lokpal Bill—of course, within the country's constitutional framework and by preserving Parliament's supremacy. I said the issues Hazare had raised were 'genuine' and 'important' and that the leadership must 'seize the moment' and 'demonstrate commitment'.

I believe that the moral authority to govern vests with the PM. The overall state of the nation is reflective of the functioning of the PM and his administration. While Dr Singh was preoccupied with saving the coalition, which took a toll on governance, Modi seemed to have employed a rather autocratic style of governance during his first term, as seen by the bitter relationship among the government, the legislature and the judiciary. Only time will tell if there is a better understanding on such matters in the second term of this government. It is also important for the government to keep in mind the demands and aspirations of the section of the population that has not voted for it, because the government represents and belongs to all sections of the people, regardless of their voting preference. Policies and programmes have to be crafted for the benefit of all.

ISSUES AFFECTING OUR BODY POLITIC

Criminalization of politics is a matter of grave concern. Introducing transparency in the funding of political parties, ensuring that the funds of political parties are subjected to regular audits and having effective legal measures in place are important steps in this direction. All political parties must hold internal organizational elections as per their rules and constitution, and candidates with criminal backgrounds should not be allowed to participate in the electoral process. It should be the collective responsibility of all political parties to take every required step for restoring what Jawaharlal Nehru called the 'majesty of Parliament'. But I also believe that this is an issue that must be dealt with pragmatically and objectively, not subjectively. The rule of law, and not general perception, must prevail. For instance, a member must be disqualified from contesting elections only if he or she is found guilty by the law of the land, and not on the mere basis of media-led allegations or charges framed against him or her. Fortunately, a law is now in place to ensure this.

The early passage of the Women's Reservation Bill to give adequate representation to women in Parliament and legislative assemblies is in the interest of the nation. However, it would require a major constitutional amendment, like it was done in the case of GST. Considering that this reservation is not exclusively for the exploited or the deprived class, the decision would be tantamount to a change in the basic structure of the Constitution. It is important that all MPs consider these aspects carefully, without being swayed by their interactions with social activists, who are constantly pushing for the women's quota.

In April 2017, a Congress-led delegation with several leaders including Sonia Gandhi, Rahul Gandhi, Satyavrat Chaturvedi and the Leader of Opposition in the Rajya Sabha, Ghulam Nabi Azad, among others, submitted a memorandum on the alleged irregularities in electronic voting machines (EVMs). I have always reiterated my faith in this system since it has a host of advantages: for one, it saves time and effort in the counting of votes. Theoretically, one cannot completely rule out the manipulation of EVMs and questions can be raised about the intent and source of manipulation. However, it is difficult to understand the interest that civil servants entrusted to conduct elections would have in indulging in such malpractices. Also, it is very difficult, if not impossible, to plan and execute electoral malpractices in a country as large and diverse as India. However, if such allegations are supported by evidence, it is for the government of the day to prove beyond any doubt the efficacy and incorruptibility of the system.

One of the methods the Constitution provides to the

executive for enacting laws is the ordinance route. I firmly believe that ordinances must be resorted to only in very compelling cases, and not too frequently. There should be no recourse to ordinance in monetary matters. Also, subjects that are already under the consideration of parliamentary panels or have been introduced in the House should not be brought in through an ordinance. If the issue is deemed urgent by the government and the matter is already before a parliamentary committee, the parliamentary panel must be taken into confidence before an ordinance is proclaimed.

THE MAKING OF LOK BHAVAN

PM Modi once tweeted that under my presidentship, Rashtrapati Bhavan had become a 'Lok Bhavan'. He reiterated that a treasure of historical documentation had come up during my tenure. I always believed that Rashtrapati Bhavan belonged to the people of India and should be thrown open to them. I was of the opinion that its beauty and majesty symbolizing the hopes and aspirations of a billion-plus people must be preserved, and that it must showcase the best that the country had to offer in science, technology, innovation and the performing arts. It was a matter of deep satisfaction to me that over 60 lakh people visited Rashtrapati Bhavan during my presidency.

As the president of the country, I never gave in to the temptation of using my so-called power, since I had no such 'power'. The 42nd Constitutional Amendment Act 1976 clearly stipulates that 'there shall be a council of Ministers with the Prime Minister at the head to aid and advise the president who shall, in the exercise of his functions, act in accordance with such advice.' Every act of the president, therefore, is on the advice of the cabinet. It was a fact that even PM Manmohan Singh was aware of, and hence did not generally approach me for advice or guidance on specific issues of governance, after I left the government.

But there were instances when several political parties made an attempt to seek advice, thus transforming Rashtrapati Bhavan into a true Lok Bhavan. I made it amply clear to them that I had finished with the discharge of my political responsibilities with my departure from North Block. On one occasion, Sonia Gandhi sought my advice regarding whether the Congress should be given the post of the leader of the Opposition. I pointed out to her that according to Parliament rules, the largest Opposition party in the House had to have at least 10 per cent of the total strength of the Lok Sabha, or 55 seats, to be eligible for that post. In my interactions with Rahul Gandhi and Ahmed Patel, who consulted me on crucial legislations such as on land acquisition law, I explained the significance of the law to them.

Delhi Chief Minister (CM) Arvind Kejriwal and his deputy, Manish Sisodia, sought my advice on the important subject of the quality of education in our schools and the introduction of special curriculum on happiness. I used one of these occasions to speak my mind to Kejriwal on his penchant for sitting on dharna over frivolous issues. He had been prone to take to the streets to highlight various concerns. On one occasion, he had even refused to leave the Lt. Governor's residence in protest against what he believed was the Lt. Governor's refusal to heed his plea, and spent a night at the place! I told him that, while all this was fine when he was an activist, if he persisted with the same strategy as CM, it would not add to the dignity of the high office he occupied. I advised that it was important for him to maintain that dignity. I can say that my conversation with him on the importance of balancing power with responsibility did lead to some turnaround in his conduct.

During the last few years of the Congress-led UPA rule, there were briefings from almost all cabinet ministers, Parliamentary Affairs minister and the PM. I heard them patiently but refused to intervene.

CHAPTER 2

ELECTIONS 2014: NOT A TURNING POINT, BUT HISTORIC

The 2014 general elections have often been described as a turning point in the evolution of our democratic polity. I do not subscribe to this view because general elections in any democracy are a normal political activity. Every Lok Sabha election has its importance because the issues that are debated during the polls reflect the various views and perceptions of the electorate. That said, the 2014 verdict was historic for two reasons. First, after three decades, a contesting political party received a decisive mandate instead of a fractured one. The last such decisive mandate was received in 1984 in the shadow of Indira Gandhi's assassination and the succession by her son, Rajiv Gandhi. Thereafter, in the elections of 1989, 1991, 1996, 1998, 1999, 2004 and 2009, no political party or group of political parties received an absolute majority in the Lok Sabha. Though the Congress under the leadership of Narasimha Rao formed the government in 1991 without the participation of any other party, it had to depend on the outside support of other political parties for its continuation in office.

The second reason is that the BJP emerged with a simple majority on its own in the Lok Sabha for the first time and was thus able to form the government, though it still did so by co-opting its allies. But the real winner was the electorate that came out in large numbers and voted decisively, thus indicating its preference for political stability, which it believed would result in development-oriented politics.

I do not think there is any co-relation between my pre-election desire for a decisive mandate, leading to a strong government (which was outlined in my speech on the eve of Republic Day on 25 January that year), and the final outcome of the elections.

In my address, I had expressed the need for a clear mandate in the forthcoming elections, as I believe that a fractured government, hostage to whimsical opportunists, is always an unhappy eventuality. In 2014, it could have been catastrophic as it was indeed a precipice moment in our history. I had said in my address, 'Each of us is a voter; each one of us has a deep responsibility; we cannot let India down.' I truly felt that it was a time of introspection and action for us.

Elsewhere in the address I stated, 'Elections do not give any person the licence to flirt with illusions. Those who seek the trust of voters must promise only what is possible. Government is not a charity shop. Populist anarchy cannot be a substitute for governance.'

Of course, people may say that the voters responded to my advice and gave a conclusive mandate in favour of PM Modi to form a government on his own. But there is no escaping the fact that the Congress had failed miserably to fulfil people's expectations and aspirations. In fact, after the campaign, when all the formalities were complete, several important Congress leaders and ministers met me at Rashtrapati Bhavan for various reasons. Interestingly, none of them expected a clear majority for either the Congress or the UPA combine. Their assessment of the number of seats that the Congress could win varied from 110 to 170.

It was not just the Congress leaders and ministers who were uncertain about a majority in the party's favour; none of the then Opposition leaders, including members of the BJP, made a realistic assessment of the number of seats the BJP would win in the elections. Only Piyush Goyal, the then national treasurer of the party and now a cabinet minister, was confident that the BJP would get no less than 265 seats, and that the number could go up to 280. I didn't and still don't know the reasons for his optimism. However, I took him seriously when he gave me Modi's detailed electioneering schedule, which was not only gruelling but also painstaking. It covered the entire length and breadth of the country.

If we were to analyze BJP's performance in earlier elections, the party got more than 180 seats in 1998 and 1999. Ever since its establishment in 1951, the Bharatiya Jana Sangh, the predecessor party of BJP, grew from strength to strength. As a component of the Janata Party, it won more than 90 seats and emerged as one of the largest groups within the Janata Party in the general elections in 1977.

Yet, I did not believe that the Congress would perform so poorly. Even in the elections after the Emergency in 1977, while the Congress faced its worst defeat in 30 years, it still managed to win 154 of the 492 seats it contested on, with a vote percentage of 34.52. But when the 2014 results were announced, it was clear that the Congress had failed to face the BJP's onslaught under Modi's leadership in nearly every part of the country, ending up with a tally of a mere 44 seats.

There has been talk that the decisive mandate the people gave, both in 2014 and 2019, signals the end of coalition politics. This is not true. Coalitions are still existent. Although the BJP won a majority on its own in 2014 and 2019, it formed the government at the Centre, in alliance with other parties comprising the NDA. But yes, a single-party majority is now a reality.

IMPORTANT LESSONS

I strongly believe that people were dejected with coalitions and the behaviour of political parties changing sides for parochial gains. Coalitions are often formed with the only common agenda of blocking a particular party or individual from coming to power. The collapse of governments from 1989 was due to irrational intra-party rivalries based on individual ambitions, whims and caprices of leaders. Sometimes coalition partners join the group while being fully aware of the ground realities, but after joining they seek to change those very realities, thus creating a crisis. For instance, in 1977, it suddenly dawned on socialist leaders like Madhu Limaye that the components of the Janata Party should not have dual membership, indicating that the Jana Sangh component of the Janata Party should not have membership of the Rashtriya Swayamsevak Sangh (RSS). It is difficult to understand the reasons for the origin of this issue at that point in time. It seemed to be aimed at destroying the Janata Party. Anyone with some knowledge of Indian political history is aware that the Jana Sangh was closely linked with the RSS. Despite these links, the Jana Sangh was accepted into the Janata Party. The decision to raise the dual membership issue, especially after a year of government formation, was definitely politically motivated and aimed at damaging the coalition.

Yet another collapse that was orchestrated was the fall of the V.P. Singh-led coalition over the issue of the construction of the Ram temple in Ayodhya. It was not clear if there was any supposed understanding between the V.P. Singh-led Janata Dal and the Vajpayee-led BJP, or the nature and implementation of that understanding. The lack of clarity meant that people were completely unhappy with the way coalition governments were formed, and the manner in which they functioned and performed.

In fact, there is a big difference in the way the UPA-I and UPA-II coalitions were formed. In 2004, UPA-I would not have come into existence without the support of the Left parties and the Samajwadi Party (SP). Both of them supported the government from outside, even though the Left took keen interest in formulating the Common Minimum Programme, on the basis of which the coalition government functioned. Many small parties were also invited to be a part of this coalition, including Ram Vilas Paswan's Lok Janshakti Party (LJP) and the Indian Union Muslim League (IUML). When the Left parties withdrew support, the Confidence Motion moved by Manmohan Singh survived in the Lok Sabha mainly with the support of the Samajwadi Party. When UPA-II was formed, many of the earlier partners such as the Left, Rashtriya Janata Dal and Janata Dal (United) [JD(U)] were not part of the coalition. Instead, Mamata Banerjee joined with 19 members of the Lok Sabha from the Trinamool Congress. But she also did not continue her support to the UPA-II for long. Even after having allied with the Congress in West Bengal in the Lok Sabha elections of 2009 and in the Assembly polls of 2011, she withdrew support from UPA-II in September 2012, despite being one of its important members. This was followed by the Dravida Munnetra Kazhagam (DMK) withdrawing its support to the coalition in March 2013. Except for the Nationalist Congress Party (NCP) and Jharkhand Mukti Morcha (JMM), none of the other regional parties supported the coalition. Therefore, it came as no surprise that the UPA-II government was unable to deliver the goods owing to the policy paralysis that had gripped it. Several crucial issues that needed to be implemented could not be executed owing to the fractious and opportunist policies of some partners.

LEADERSHIP IN TIMES OF CRISIS

Some members of the Congress have theorized that, had I become the PM in 2004, the party might have averted the 2014 Lok Sabha drubbing. Though I don't subscribe to this view, I do believe that the party's leadership lost political focus after my elevation as president. While Sonia Gandhi was unable to handle the affairs of the party, Dr Singh's prolonged absence from the House put an end to any personal contact with other MPs. During my days in the Rajya Sabha, I managed to develop close links with several leaders like Mulayam Singh Yadav and Mayawati.

In fact, Mayawati's personal affinity for me ensured her support during the presidential election, much to the chagrin of the SP supremo. Besides, some senior Congress leaders' political naiveté and arrogance hurt the fortunes of the party further.

I believe that the leadership of a party in times of crisis has to evolve a different approach. If I had continued in the government as finance minister, I would have ensured Mamata's continuity in the coalition. Similarly, Maharashtra was handled badly, partly due to decisions taken by Sonia Gandhi. I would have brought back Shivraj Patil or Sushil Kumar Shinde, considering the dearth of a strong leader from the state, like Vilasrao Deshmukh. I don't think I would have allowed the state of Telangana to be created. I firmly believe that my presence in active politics would have ensured that the Congress wouldn't have faced the drubbing it received in the 2014 general elections.

PREPARING FOR POLLS

The pre-election period of 2013–14 was marked by economic instability. Further, the precarious scenario in the immediate neighbourhood, characterized by the instability in Afghanistan, the fear of communist reprisal in Nepal and the rise of nascent democracy in Bhutan, forced me to look at the external dimensions of the looming elections.

The chief election commissioner came to me with the schedule recommended by the government. Based on the advice of the PM through the Election Commission of India, I issued the order as president to hold the Lok Sabha elections. Thereafter, the model code of conduct was enforced and I was out of the picture. I refrained from exercising my voting right in the general elections as I had been voted to the constitutional post of president by a number of parties and firmly believed that it would be incorrect for me to vote for a certain party or candidate.

I appointed T.K. Viswanathan, former union law secretary and former secretary-general of the Lok Sabha, to be my advisor on all post-poll presidential decisions. As the president is the supreme authority while choosing the PM immediately after the general election, I did not want to be vulnerable if a post-election scenario called for my intervention as an arbiter. I wanted to be in a position to take a considered view of appropriate action in any given situation. I made sure I was guided by the transition of governments in various countries.

I had expected a hung Parliament with the BJP emerging as the single largest party with about 195–200 seats. In such a situation, it would have been my constitutional responsibility to ensure stability. Had the Congress emerged with fewer seats but promised a stable government, I would have invited the leader of the party to form the government, keeping in mind their previous track record in managing coalition governments successfully. This would have been in contravention of the convention established by the former president, Shankar Dayal Sharma, of inviting the single-largest party to form the government. He had invited Vajpayee to form the government after a hung House in 1996, despite lack of clarity on Vajpayee's numbers. I was convinced even before the 2014 elections that I would not be neutral between stability and instability. It was this sentiment that was amply evident in my Republic Day address to the nation in January 2014.

DAY OF RECKONING

The day of the results, 16 May 2014, was just like any other day, as far as I was concerned. I directed my aide-de-camp (ADC) to keep me informed of the trends every half an hour. When the results were finally announced later that evening, I was greatly relieved over the decisive mandate but also disappointed at my one-time party's performance. It was difficult to believe that the Congress had managed to win just 44 seats. The Congress is a national institution interlinked with people's lives. Its future is always a concern of every thinking individual.

There were many reasons for its defeat. I feel that the party failed to recognize the end of its charismatic leadership. Tall leaders like Pandit Nehru ensured that India, unlike Pakistan, survived and developed into a strong and stable nation. Sadly, such extraordinary leaders are not there anymore, reducing the establishment to a government of averages.

MEETING THE PM-DESIGNATE

My first interaction with the PM-designate Narendra Modi was during a formal meeting with BJP leaders L.K. Advani, Rajnath Singh, Murli Manohar Joshi, Sushma Swaraj and Arun Jaitley. Rajnath informed me of the party's resolution along with the letters of support and requested me to formally invite Modi to form the government. I congratulated Modi, who requested for some time to speak with me. Using a newspaper clipping that had reported on my earlier speech hoping for a politically stable mandate, he asserted that he had achieved the objective of a clear majority that I had envisaged. Thereafter, he requested for a week's time before the swearing-in ceremony. I was surprised at his request. He insisted that he needed time to address the issue of his successor in his home state, Gujarat. He, however, confirmed to me that he had no such problems in cabinet formation at the Centre.

Modi then sought my advice on his intent to invite all the heads of state/government of the South Asian Association for Regional Cooperation (SAARC) countries for the swearing-in ceremony. I complimented him on the idea and advised him to discuss the same with the head of the Intelligence Bureau, owing to the enormous security risks facing leaders of Afghanistan, Pakistan and Sri Lanka.

I have had very cordial relations with PM Modi during my tenure. However, I did not hesitate to give my advice on matters of policy during our meetings. There were several occasions when he echoed concerns that I had voiced. I also believe that he has managed to grasp the nuances of foreign policy quickly.

Ahead of the 2019 elections, I did not have any advice for the Congress, having quit the government years ago. However, I did believe that there was a possibility of a coalition government coming to power in 2019, which could be either a pre- or post-poll alliance. I am convinced that Indian democracy is resilient, and the electorate is wiser than any individual or party. The voters have never failed this country. Eventually, Modi returned with even bigger numbers than he had in 2014, but still proceeded to form a coalition government with the BJP's pre-poll allies.

CHAPTER 3

OF PRESIDENTIAL ADDRESSES: BOTH CANDID AND CAUTIOUS

The President of India normally addresses the nation on ceremonial occasions, such as on the eve of Republic Day and Independence Day. The PM unfurls the national flag at Red Fort, a practice that was initiated in 1947, on Independence Day. It's an honour that many would aspire for. The likes of Charan Singh and H.D. Deve Gowda had often spoken of the dream of a 'farmer's son' unfurling the national flag from the ramparts of Red Fort. The president, on the other hand, marks the event by hosting a reception at his official residence, Rashtrapati Bhavan. This is popularly known as 'At Home', which is held in the evening. In the morning, he places a wreath at the Amar Jawan Jyoti in New Delhi in honour of martyred soldiers. Around the same time, he also felicitates freedom fighters in Rashtrapati Bhavan. These important events—conducted in an elaborate, ceremonial manner—are eagerly anticipated by the invitees. Being honoured by the President of India is an accomplishment that is treasured by them for life.

Rajendra Prasad, our first president, said in his address after the country was formally declared a republic, that 'India has had a long and chequered history; parts of it were cloudy and parts bright and sunlit'. He pointed out that it was the first time in the country's long civilizational history that the entire nation had been 'brought under one Constitution and one rule'. Speaking of the cultural ties that our ancestors had forged with the rest of the world, Prasad said that 'our ties subsist because they were not of iron and steel or even of gold, but of the silken chords of the human spirit'. Referring to the Constitution as a 'democratic instrument', he stated that we would be 'implementing in practice under our Constitution what we have inherited from our traditions, namely, freedom of opinion and expression'. His speech was in keeping with the mood of those days, when the country was in happy anticipation of the fruits of freedom. It also underlined the absolute need to sustain the values of free speech, tolerance and malice towards none, which had been an inherent part of our ancient civilization.

The tenure of Dr S. Radhakrishnan in Rashtrapati Bhavan witnessed moments of tension and grief. Two wars broke out, in 1962 and 1965; and two PMs died—Nehru in 1964 and Lal Bahadur Shastri in 1966. But during all those troubled times, Dr Radhakrishnan stood out as a beacon of courage and fortitude, instilling in the country self-confidence and self-respect. In his last Republic Day address as president, he observed:

> It is said that our country consists of the whole geographical area bounded by the Himalayas in the North and the sea

in the South. All those who live within the limits of India are Indian, whatever may be their race, caste or community. There was practically free trade in the matter of ideas, beliefs, and customs. But, unfortunately, we have not yet developed an 'All-India' outlook. We fight with each other for petty considerations and regional advantages. Such minor interests will have to be subordinated to the larger national good.

I have mentioned the above instance to underline that our past presidents had raised issues and concerns that reflected the mood of the nation then. Thereafter, successive presidents too have spoken, either in Parliament or outside, on issues that had seized the country.

I realized that the more we changed as a nation, the more our concerns remained the same. As I mentioned in my acceptance speech, a modern nation is built on some basic fundamentals: democracy, or equal rights for every citizen; secularism, or equal freedom to every faith; equality of every region and language; gender equality; and, perhaps most important of all, economic equity. For our development to be real, the poorest of our land must feel that they are part of the narrative of rising India.

The president's speech on such and other historic occasions has often been a talking point and has at times led to some controversy. This has given rise to several questions. Should the president be free to speak what he wishes to, even if it embarrasses the government? Should he get his speech transcript cleared from the government beforehand? Should the government actually prepare the address that the president is to deliver? I wish to make one thing clear: I have never shown my speech before any event to any official of the government. But at the same time, I have refrained from being reckless or populist, taking care not to say anything against the government policies and programmes. Theoretically and constitutionally, the president is the 'creator' of the Union government, by virtue of the fact that he appoints the PM and other ministers on the PM's advice, and administers oath of office to them. Logically, therefore, it would appear that the president has every right or power to criticize his government. He can publicly disapprove of a particular action or mention acts of omission and commission.

I have often reasoned with myself on this matter, bringing into play various aspects: If, as a president, I felt so strongly, someone could well ask me: 'Why are you then not dismissing the government? After all, the president is the appointing authority.' I would have no answer. Thus, I had to be careful and calibrated in my addresses. It was, therefore, only proper that I didn't condemn or criticize the government in the public domain through my Independence Day or Republic Day addresses, although I never shied away from taking up issues of contemporary concerns. At the same time, I maintained a level of independence—one, by not showing my speech beforehand to the government; and two, by exercising my right to advice the government behind closed doors on matters where I thought it ought to take corrective measures. My addresses were of hope, encouragement and a desire to see the government improve its performance. Here, I did not mince words.

A few things that I said in these addresses became quite popular and even quotable in later days for their relevance. Take, for instance, my observations in the Republic Day speech I delivered in 2014, a few months ahead of the general elections. My message that year was a call to more than 800 million electors to vote for political stability and not for fragile coalitions. The message was without doubt a bit political and out of tune with the normal messages on such occasions, but I deliberately chose to do so as I felt that it was my responsibility as the first citizen of the country to advise my fellow citizens to discharge their rights with responsibility.

These were my reflections on the political situation prevalent then, and I had not consulted anyone in the government (UPA-II) while drafting them. As I was to know soon, the voter seemed to have been thinking precisely on the same lines, and the electorate gave a clear mandate to a party to rule. Although that party, the BJP, still went ahead and formed a coalition government, it was not dependent on the whims and fancies of alliance partners.

But when it came to the contents of the speech that I delivered to joint sessions of Parliament, I scrupulously left it to the government to provide a draft. In such cases, as president, I was at liberty to offer my suggestions and insights to the draft, and then I left it to the President's Secretariat and the PM's Office (PMO) to collaborate and prepare a final text. The president's address to the joint sessions of Parliament reflects the aims, aspirations and policies of the government of the day. Because I followed the rule book and conventions in both letter and spirit and also did not shy away from offering suggestions at the appropriate fora, there was not a single occasion in the five years of my tenure as president that my addresses created a controversy or embarrassed the government of the day. However, on one occasion, I accepted a compromise on my original text, on the advice of the PM. In the run-up address to the Republic Day of 2013, I had, in the text I prepared, dealt in detail with the horrific Nirbhaya rape-and-murder case. PM Manmohan Singh gently advised me against an elaboration of the incident. Given the prevailing situation, I thought it was a wise suggestion and accepted it. Barring this speech, I never had issues with the UPA government in my other speeches relating to Republic Day and Independence Day, from 2012 to 2014.

While on the Nirbhaya case, I must mention that some people had sought an audience with me, even as a large number of people had come out on the streets in protest against the incident and in condemnation of both the state and the union governments. Perhaps they wanted me to be actively involved in the issue. I had declined to meet them, because I was clear in my mind that the issue had to be handled by the union home minister. The incident was no doubt ghastly and it had troubled my conscience as well, but the country's president had to demonstrate calm and dignity that behoved the high office he held. I was certainly not abdicating my responsibility. I would like to narrate an incident to demonstrate my point. My wife had passed away in August 2015 and three hours before her cremation, I was scheduled to meet a business delegation—an appointment that had been finalized several days before. I could have opted out of the appointment given the personal tragedy, but state business cannot wait, unless the president is physically unwell. I kept that appointment.

BEHIND THE SCENES

I generally prepared the text of my speeches both on the basis of the inputs I received from the government as well as from my own understanding of the situation of the time, as I earlier mentioned. I worked hard on my speeches, sharing my thoughts with my secretary for them to be drafted and included in the address. This would be followed by preliminary discussions with senior officials. I would also receive inputs from learned friends whom I reached out to, but always made sure that I spoke in generalities and not about specifics. Care had to be taken to bring in nuances; the speech must reflect the reality on the ground and at the same time suggest a way ahead. A first draft would then be prepared based on the exercise conducted, which I would dictate to a stenographer. Then there were rehearsals, during which officials made sure that all extraneous noises were cut out. They also made sure that I wore a dress whose colour was studio-friendly. At times I read with the aid of a teleprompter. The last bit was a problem in the beginning. I was used to speaking extempore and took time to adjust to the teleprompter. The freedom to choose words gets severely restricted when one reads from a prepared text.

My first address to the nation was from a studio and it came in a year in which, for the most part, I had been a minister in the government. It was quite a challenge. I was very conscious about the public reaction to the speech. Besides, I didn't have much time for preparation; it was less than three weeks after I became president that I had to deliver the Independence Day address. Most of my time was consumed in receiving congratulatory messages and telephone calls from heads of state all over the world. It was only around 7–8 August that I began work on the address. I took the trouble of reading the speeches of some of my predecessors and getting a grasp of the exercise. I also had to carefully choose the topics on which I spoke, given that the PM would also be speaking on a wide range of subjects during his customary speech from the ramparts of the Red Fort.

In 2012, I spoke of the economic challenges the country faced, the Eurozone crisis, declining exports and fall in investments. But I also expressed optimism on economic growth based on material available from various credible sources. I noted how India had slipped in industrial and economic growth during the British period and how it first took baby steps to recover and then launched into an overdrive of growth. Here is what I said:

> In 1750, seven years before the fateful Battle of Plassey, India had 24.5 per cent of world manufacturing output and Britain had risen to 18.5 per cent. The western industrial revolution was in its incipient stages in the 18th century, but even in this regard, India slipped from seven to one in per capita industrialization in that period, while Britain vaulted from 10 to 100. Between 1900 and 1947, India's economic growth rate was an annual average of 1 per cent. From such depths, we climbed, first to 3 per cent growth, and then took a quantum leap forward: today, despite two great international crises that rocked the world and some domestic dips, we have posted an average growth rate of more than 8 per cent over the last seven years.

I quoted former president and academic S. Radhakrishnan, who said: 'Economic progress is one of the tests of democracy.'

I mentioned the changed political scenario in the address to the nation on the eve of the 2015 Republic Day and expressed hope that India would march to prosperity for all. I said,

> The past year has been remarkable in many ways. Particularly because, after three decades, the people have voted to power a single party with a majority for a stable government, and in the process, freed the country's governance from the compulsions of coalition politics... The voter has played her part; it is now up to those who have been elected to honour this trust. It was a vote for clean, efficient, effective, gender-sensitive, transparent, accountable and citizen-friendly governance.

I also took the occasion to remind everyone concerned about the need for a robust legislature:

> The legislature reflects the will of the people. It is the platform where progressive legislation using civilized dialogue must create delivery mechanisms for realising the aspirations of the people... Enacting laws without discussion impacts the law-making role of Parliament. It breaches the trust reposed in it by the people. This is neither good for the democracy nor for the policies relating to those laws.

I also sounded a warning on sectarian conflicts, saying that the much-talked-of soft power that India has and hopes to wield, cannot be effective unless we follow the wise saying, 'Unity is strength; dominance is weakness': 'Much is said about India's soft power. But the most powerful example of India's soft power in an international environment where so many countries are sinking into the morass of theocratic violence, lies in our definition of the relationship between faith and polity.'

My fifth address to the nation was on the eve of Independence Day in 2016, in which I commended the ruling and the Opposition parties for coming together in the pursuit of a national agenda for development, unity and integrity of the nation. I hailed the non-partisan approach of all parties in the passage of the Constitution Amendment Bill for the introduction of the GST. But then, I also voiced my concern over the rise of divisive and intolerant forces in parts of the country, especially the attacks on weaker sections of society, including the Dalits, and flagged the crisis in agriculture:

> In these four years, I also saw with some disquiet, forces of divisiveness and intolerance trying to raise their ugly head. Attacks on weaker sections that militate against our national ethos are aberrations that need to be dealt with firmly. The collective wisdom of our society and our polity gives me the confidence that such forces will remain marginalized and India's remarkable growth story will continue uninterrupted.

In addition, I once again harped on the need for a functioning legislature, saying that that 'disruptions, obstructionism and unmindful pursuit of a divisive political agenda by groups and individuals lead to nothing by institutional travesty and constitutional subversion'.

ADDRESS TO PARLIAMENT

My speech in Parliament at the start of the Budget Session in 2015 reflected the promises the Modi government had made to the people and the steps it had taken in the direction of inclusive growth. The government had taken charge barely a year ago and there was optimism and trust in the air. Underlining the new slogan of the regime, I said that 'the fundamental tenet of my government is *sabka saath, sabka vikas* (support from all, development for all).' The session was especially important because it was then that the Modi government presented its first full-year Union Budget. I spoke of the various initiatives the government had taken for inclusive growth, such as the Pradhan Mantri Jan Dhan Yojana, the Direct Benefit Transfer programme and the Swachh Bharat Abhiyan. My address also mentioned the government's ambitious plan to provide electricity, housing and toilets to all in a committed time-frame. I spoke of various programmes and policies the government had framed to benefit the farmers. The government had also initiated an amended land acquisition law, named the Right to Fair Compensation and Transparency in Land Acquisition, Rehabilitation and Resettlement Act. However, reforms in the land acquisition process have remained a non-starter for a variety of reasons.

My 2015 speech was drafted by the government of the day, and it referred to the establishment of the National Institution for Transforming India, or NITI Aayog, to take the place of the Planning Commission. I stated that the new body was meant to 'foster the spirit of cooperative federalism so that the Union and the state governments come on a platform to forge a common national agenda for development, with a thrust on empowering the impoverished'. While I was personally not enthused by the scrapping of the Planning Commission, which had been established in 1950, I did not wish to rake up a controversy by opposing it publicly. I personally feel it was a mistake, indeed a blunder, to do away with the plan panel.

Of course, the Planning Commission's long tenure was not without controversies. Often there were tiffs between the government and the plan panel, even during the Nehru era. Besides, I believe that transitions must be done in a smooth manner and with a human face. The Planning Commission had been set up as an advisory body through a Cabinet resolution, and it assumed extraordinary powers through the allocation of funds to states. It derived its strength from the Mahalanobis Model, named after the famous economist P.C. Mahalanobis—founder of the Indian Statistical Institute and a close aide of Jawaharlal Nehru. Mahalanobis believed in state-directed investments, emphasis on heavy industries and public sector undertakings, and a generally centralized economy. While some of these concepts may sound dated today, in the early years of independence they served the country well, since they provided our policy planners a long-term growth road map through Five-Year Plans (FYPs), which the Planning Commission of India was tasked with preparing. Interestingly, the Mahalanobis Model was introduced in India after the first FYP (1951–56). The first plan was based on what is known as the Harrod-Domar Model, which argued that production required capital; capital is gathered through investments; and the faster one accumulates capital, the greater growth would be. But Mahalanobis differed with this line of thinking and pointed to the constraints of economy in managing such growth. His opinion prevailed from the second plan onward.

My address to the joint session of Parliament in 2017 came against the backdrop of the government's decision to advance the Budget cycle and the merger of the Railway Budget with the general Budget for the first time in independent India. I took pride in speaking of women empowerment—*nari shakti*—and gave the example of the grand performance of Indian sportswomen P.V. Sindhu, Sakshi Malik, Deepa Karmakar and others. I mentioned that women were being inducted into the combat streams of our armed forces, and spoke of the first three women fighter pilots.

In the course of these various addresses, I touched upon a host of other subjects as well. I spoke of India's rise as an important power and a leader in innovation and start-ups; its achievements in areas of infrastructure, poverty alleviation, education and health; the need to nurture the symbiotic relationship between man and nature; the importance of International Yoga Day; various government initiatives such as the Clean India mission, Skill India, Make in India, Digital India; and the many housing and electrification schemes for the poor, especially those living in rural India. I also spoke of the need to firmly deal with Left-Wing Extremism and terrorism. I referred to some path-breaking legislation such as those that protect children from sexual offences and women from harassment at the workplace. I emphasized repeatedly the need to preserve and promote our democratic institutions and the importance of a functioning legislature to governance and democracy.

Having delivered several speeches during my term as

president, I believe that many of my observations were taken into consideration by the government of the day. Yet, there were some that were not adequately addressed. For instance, not enough attention has been paid to my warning on attacks on the less privileged sections of society and minorities. I have also been uneasy over the attempt by a section of the establishment to erase the legacy of Nehru, who played a stellar role in establishing and strengthening the country's various democratic institutions.

FAREWELL SPEECH

My farewell speech in Parliament in July 2017 as president was a mix of nostalgia and present-day realities. I recalled that I had first entered Parliament back in July 1969, as a Rajya Sabha member from West Bengal. Since then, on various occasions, I served as an MP both from the Rajya Sabha and the Lok Sabha and in ministerial positions.

I paid tributes to Indira Gandhi who had mentored my career as a parliamentarian, and had a steely resolve, whether in success or adversity. I recounted an incident when I had accompanied Mrs Gandhi to London after the post-Emergency electoral defeat she and her party had encountered. When one of the journalists asked her opinion on the lessons she had learned, she promptly said: 'In those 21 months, we comprehensively managed to alienate all sections of the Indian people.'

I had also been deeply influenced by stalwarts such as M.C. Chagla, Bhupesh Gupta and Joachim Alva, and I named them and various others in my speech. I also expressed my indebtedness to stalwarts P.V. Narasimha Rao, Madhu Limaye, Atal Bihari Vajpayee,

Dr Manmohan Singh and L.K. Advani, from whom I learned a lot in my years as a parliamentarian. About PM Modi I remarked,

> As I had said on oath, I strived to preserve, protect and defend our Constitution, not just in word but also in spirit. In this task, I greatly benefitted from the advice and cooperation extended to me by Prime Minister Modi at every step. With passion and energy, he is driving transformational changes in the country. I will carry with me fond memories of our association and his warm and courteous behaviour.

I flagged two important issues in my farewell speech: The declining number of days Parliament conducted meaningful business, and the need to use the ordinance route to a minimum. I said: 'It is unfortunate that the parliamentary time devoted to legislation has been declining. With the heightened complexity of administration, legislation must be preceded by scrutiny and adequate discussion on the floor of the House.' On ordinances, I stated that through the instrument of ordinances, the executive has been vested with extraordinary powers to make laws to meet exigencies during a time when Parliament is not in session. However, such ordinances have to be approved by Parliament within six weeks of its next session.

> I am firm in the opinion that the ordinance route should be used only in compelling circumstances and there should be no recourse to ordinances on monetary matters. The ordinance route should not be taken on matters which are being considered or have been introduced in the House or a committee of the House. If a matter is deemed urgent,

the concerned committee should be made aware of the situation and should be mandated to present its report within the stipulated time.

In my final address to the nation, I thanked the citizens of India for their trust and confidence in me. I said,

> Five years ago, when I took the oath of office of the President of the Republic, I promised to preserve, protect and defend our Constitution, not just in word but also in spirit. Each day of these five years, I was conscious of my responsibility. I learnt from my travels across the length and breadth of the country. I learnt from my conversations with young and bright minds in colleges and universities, scientists, innovators, scholars, jurists, authors, artists and leaders from across the spectrum. These interactions kept me focused and inspired. I strove hard. How successful I was in discharging my responsibilities will be judged, over the time, by the critical lens of history. As one advances in years, so does one's propensity to sermonize. But I have no sermon to make. For the past fifty years of my public life, my sacred text has been the Constitution of India, my temple has been the Parliament of India, and my passion has been the service of the people of India.

I also raised the issue of the growing spectre of violence in our society and underlined that it militated against our civilizational values.

> The capacity for compassion and empathy is the true foundation of our civilization. But every day, we see

increased violence around us. At the heart of this violence is darkness, fear and mistrust. We must free our public discourse from all forms of violence, physical as well as verbal. Only a non-violent society can ensure the participation of all sections of the people, especially the marginalized and the dispossessed in the democratic process. Power of non-violence has to be resurrected to build a compassionate and caring society.

The need to strike a balance between development and environmental protection has been the topic of debate for decades. This has been especially relevant in a developing economy such as that of India. While acknowledging the need for growth, I emphasized on the difference between 'need' and 'greed' in the speech. I said,

> Protection of the environment is essential for our survival. Nature has been kind to us in its bounty. But when greed exceeds need, nature lets loose its fury. We often see some parts of India affected by devastating floods while others reel under severe drought. Climate change has put farming sector under tremendous stress. Scientists and technologists have to work with millions of farmers and workers to revive the health of our soil, arrest the decline in the water table and restore the ecological balance.

I have repeatedly held the view that education is a key factor in the prosperity of our country. I mentioned it in my address on assuming the office of President of India, and I raised the subject in my farewell speech as well:

Education is the alchemy that can take India to its next golden age. A reordering of society is possible through the transformative power of education. For that, we have to upgrade our higher institutions of learning to world-class levels. Our education system must accept disruption as a norm and prepare our students to manage and build upon the disruptions. Our universities should not be a place for rote-memorizing but an assembly of inquisitive minds. Creative thinking, innovation and scientific temper have to be promoted in our institutions of higher learning. It calls for application of logic through discussion, argument and analysis. These qualities have to be cultivated and autonomy of mind has to be encouraged.

On the whole, although it was an emotional address, I did not feel anything extraordinary thereafter. I took tea and attended to the large number of people waiting to meet me. However, many thoughts rushed through my mind: That I would not be entering this grand edifice, the temple of democracy, again. And, even if I did as a visitor, I would not be entering the Central Hall, which is so rich in history. And, as several people bid me goodbye, I recalled my quiet debut in Parliament 48 years ago. I was an unknown face then, and the deputy secretary of the Rajya Sabha welcomed me, as he did other newcomers.

Thereafter, I got busy with the task of vacating the official residence. Books and material in the wardrobe had to be packed.

In the days to come, a sense of vacuum gripped me. My personal staff had gone, my wife was no more and my occupancy at Rashtrapati Bhavan had come to an end. I shifted to 10,

Rajaji Marg, which had last housed A.P.J. Abdul Kalam after he retired as president. What remained was a sense of fulfilment and happiness of having served the people of this great country as their humble servant.

CHAPTER 4

ARTICLE 356 AND INDIA'S FEDERAL SPIRIT: USE AND MISUSE

Article 356 has been one of the most contentious provisions of the Constitution of India, because it equips the Centre with the powers to dismiss a state government under certain extraordinary circumstances. It has been often used (and misused) over the decades, with the victims lamenting that the federal structure of the country's parliamentary democracy had been assaulted in the process. The president has a critical role to play, since he approves the execution of the article, and can ask the government to reconsider its decision. There is merit in some of the claims made by those that are either at the receiving end of the provision or have a principled position against it, but we need to first understand what the federal structure means in the Indian context. There are presumptions here and I believe that historical facts must be objectively applied to form an informed opinion.

ON FEDERAL STRUCTURE

India had never been a federal state. The British Crown succeeded the East India Company which was, in turn, a successor state of the Mughal Empire. The successor governments of the British were those that were formed in India and Pakistan after Partition. During the British rule, the Queen had assured the princely states that they would not be annexed and would be allowed to conduct their business with riders—such as that they could not maintain an army or have independent alliances with neighbours. Besides, they came under the overall command of the Governor General. The Indian territory, which was administered by the Governor General, was divided into a number of provinces. Some of them were governed by governors and others by Lt. Governors. There were regions that were administered by chief commissioners. The British made and unmade these provinces. For instance, they partitioned Bengal in 1905 and unified it in 1911.

The control of the British over these princely states, which were never a federation in sum, was further strengthened by the Doctrine of Lapse, a policy initiated by Governor General Lord Dalhousie in 1848. Under this doctrine, a princely state faced the prospect of annexation by the imperial power if the ruler of that state was either 'manifestly incompetent or died without a male heir'. Interestingly, even before this doctrine came into being, the British East India Company had annexed many such small states. But Dalhousie's policy invigorated the process and, more pertinently, became the direct cause of the 1857 revolt— variously described as the Sepoy Mutiny by British historians or India's First War of Independence by nationalist historians.

While on the revolt, it must be recalled that the Doctrine of Lapse resulted in a direct confrontation between the British and Queen Lakshmibai of Jhansi, who had adopted a male heir, which the East Indian Company refused to recognize and made plans to annex Jhansi.

In addition, the policy of Subsidiary Alliance was refined and executed by Governor General Lord Wellesley. The doctrine, which placed the princely rulers virtually at the mercy of the British through an 'alliance', was yet another means to execute annexations. The British made a serious attempt at making India a federation through the Government of India Act, 1935. It was mandated to make 'further provision for the Government of India'; it received the Royal Assent in July 1935 and commenced in April 1937. The Act is generally known for the grant of a measure of autonomy to the provinces of British India through the abolition of provincial dyarchy (some powers vested with officials responsible to the provincial legislatures and other powers with the British-appointed provincial governor), introduction of direct elections, partial reorganization of provinces, and the creation of a federal court, among other things. Importantly, the Act also provided for the establishment of a 'Federation of India' that would comprise both British India and some or all of the princely states. However, the plan to create such a federation fell apart after most of the princely states refused to endorse it; according to the law, the federation could be established only with the concurrence of at least 50 per cent of the states. Also, the outbreak of the Second World War and the changed political priorities thereafter, effectively extinguished the flame of the Indian federation the British had in mind.

Being sworn in as the 13th President of India: Chief Justice of India S.H. Kapadia administers the oath of office to me at an impressive ceremony at the historic Central Hall of Parliament in 2012.

President Pratibha Patil welcomes me at the Rashtrapati Bhavan in 2012. Also seen is her husband, Devisingh Ransingh Shekhawat.

Presenting the President's standards to the 33 Squadron of the Indian Air Force in 2012, in recognition of the exceptional service rendered by it to the nation.

Enjoying a laugh with the CM of Tamil Nadu, J. Jayalalithaa, in Chennai in 2012.

Receiving the famed Tirupati laddu after offering puja at the Tirumala Venkateswara Temple in Tirupati in 2012. Also seen is the CM of Andhra Pradesh, Kiran Kumar Reddy.

Enjoying a boat ride, along with J&K CM Omar Abdullah, on the Dal Lake in Srinagar in 2012.

Interacting with students in Punjab in 2012 (with CM Parkash Singh Badal [seated; right]).

The old guard and the new: With the CM of UP, Akhilesh Yadav (extreme left), and his father and founder of the Samajwadi Party, Mulayam Singh Yadav (to my right), in Lucknow in 2012.

Enjoying an early morning walk during my visit to Himachal Pradesh in 2013.

At the Eleventh Pravasi Bharatiya Divas in Kochi, Kerala, in 2013.

Inaugurating the Surajkund International Crafts Mela in Surajkund, Haryana, in 2013, with CM Bhupinder Singh Hooda (to my left) and Governor Jagannath Pahadia (to my right).

I am all ears as CM Bhupinder Singh Hooda speaks to me in Kurukshetra, Haryana, in 2013.

Lieutenant Commander Abhilash Tomy, the skipper of Mhadei, is all smiles as I congratulate him on the successful completion of Sagar Parikrama-II, the non-stop solo circumnavigation of the globe, in 2013. The Governor of Maharashtra, K. Sankaranarayanan (to my left), and the Chief of Naval Staff, Admiral D.K. Joshi, look on.

In an animated discussion with the CM of Rajasthan, Ashok Gehlot, and Governor Margaret Alva in Rajasthan in 2013.

Offering a chaadar (ceremonial cloth) at the dargah of Sufi saint Khwaja Moinuddin Chishti in Ajmer, Rajasthan, in 2013.

With Odisha CM Naveen Patnaik in his state in 2013.

Enjoying a meal with the Governor of Tripura, Devanand Konwar (left), and CM Manik Sarkar in Agartala in 2013.

Saluting the sacrifice of our martyrs at the war memorial in Arunachal Pradesh in 2013.

In an engaging discussion with the Governor of Sikkim, Balmiki Prasad Singh (right), and CM Pawan Kumar Chamling in Gangtok in 2013.

Visiting a market in Gangtok.

Celebrating 56 years of happiness: With my wife, Suvra, at our marriage anniversary at Rashtrapati Bhavan in 2013.

Jharkhand CM Hemant Soren and his son bid adieu as I leave after my visit to the state in 2014.

At the Holy Shrine of Mata Vaishno Devi in Jammu in 2014.

Administering the oath of office and secrecy to Narendra Modi, as the 15th Prime Minister of India, in 2014 with the majestic Rashtrapati Bhavan in the background.

With Gujarat CM, Anandiben Patel, at the Dr A.P.J. Abdul Kalam IGNITE Awards at IIM Ahmedabad in 2015.

With the CM of Mizoram, Lal Thanhawla, during a visit the state in 2015.

Durga Puja celebrations at my ancestral home in Mirati in Birbhum district, West Bengal, in 2016.

Sharing a laugh with the cadets of the prestigious Officers Training Academy, Chennai, in 2016.

Showcasing our navy to the world: With PM Narendra Modi (right), Raksha Mantri Manohar Parrikar (extreme left) and Chief of the Naval Staff, Admiral R.K. Dhowan, at the International Fleet Review at Visakhapatnam in 2016.

In conversation with Jyotiraditya Scindia at the 60th Foundation Day of the Scindia Kanya Vidyalaya, Gwalior, Madhya Pradesh, in 2016.

Paying my last respects to the CM of Tamil Nadu, J. Jayalalithaa, in Chennai in 2016.

Being welcomed to Nalanda by Bihar Governor, Ram Nath Kovind, and CM Nitish Kumar in 2017.

Amidst the majestic Himalayas in Uttarakhand in 2017.

Signing a book for Baba Ramdev in Uttarakhand in 2017.

The CM of Assam, Sarbananda Sonowal (right), and Governor Jagdish Mukhi welcome me with a japi (headgear), a traditional symbol of Assamese folk culture, in Assam, in 2017.

After offering prayers at the Kamakshi Amman Temple in Kanchipuram, Tamil Nadu, in 2017.

Interacting with students in West Bengal in 2017.

With Governor Kaptan Singh Solanki (left) and industrialist and former MP, Naveen Jindal, at Sonipat, Haryana, in 2017.

Shiv Sena Chief, Uddhav Thackeray (to my right), and his son Aaditya welcome me during my visit to Mumbai, Maharashtra, in 2017.

Rajasthan CM Vasundhara Raje shares her thoughts with me at a function in Jaipur in 2017.

Therefore, the federal system is not uniquely an Indian concept. In 1928, the Motilal Nehru Committee Report, which was a memorandum outlining a proposed new dominion status for India, had referred to a federal nature for the country's management. The report had been prepared by an All Parties Conference chaired by Motilal Nehru, with Jawaharlal Nehru as the panel's secretary. While the report spoke of a federal form of government, it also stated that residuary powers should be vested in the Centre. Many experts have since observed that the Nehru Committee report endorsed what is basically a unitary form of government rather than a federal dispensation—a strong Centre with varied powers to states. While moving the Objectives Resolution in the Constituent Assembly in December 1946 for a road map ahead of a free India, Jawaharlal Nehru said the resolution pledged for the creation of an Independent Sovereign Republic. On the concluding day of the Constituent Assembly in November 1949, B.R. Ambedkar spoke of the need to always and relentlessly protect and promote democracy and steer clear of hero-worship.

The 'federation' that the British were so eager to vest on India through the Government of India Act of 1935, was also cast aside with the Partition of India. There was never a federation of states and this was reflected in the Constitution of India, which was adopted after an extensive debate in the Constituent Assembly. Members of the Assembly discussed the issue at length, some in favour of having the term 'federal' in the Preamble to the Constitution and many others negating the idea. The language used in the Constitution set the controversy to rest. The very first provision, Article 1(1), reads: 'India, that is Bharat, shall be a Union of States.' Part XI of the Constitution deals with 'Relations between the Union and the States'; Part XIV talks of 'Services Under the Union and the States'. Nowhere is the term 'federal' or 'federation' applied. Dr Ambedkar explained the situation while submitting the draft Constitution for consideration, saying that while the Constitution was federal in structure, the drafting committee had used the term 'Union' for two important reasons: One, that the Indian federation is not the outcome of an agreement among the states; and two, component units (states) do not have the freedom to secede from the Union of India. In other words, the federal structure as we understand it today, simply refers to a broad arrangement symbolizing a healthy relationship between the Centre and the states. Over the years, federalism has taken many forms, the more recent being 'cooperative federalism' and 'competitive federalism'.

The federal concept came into focus with the formation of the States Reorganisation Commission (SRC) by the Centre in 1953. The panel was tasked to recommend the reorganization of state boundaries. Two years later, the SRC submitted its report, recommending that boundaries be reorganized to form 16 states and three union territories. The SRC report, inter alia, recommended the abolishing of the part system. Contiguity and linguistic aspects were taken into consideration in the reorganization of the states. The States Reorganisation Act was passed in Parliament and implemented from 1 November 1956. As a result of the Act, the country was reorganized into 14 states and six union territories. They were big changes: a new state of Kerala was created, Mysore state was renamed Karnataka in 1973 and Marathwada, initially with the Nizam's Hyderabad, was transferred to Bombay state, which in 1960, was divided into Maharashtra and Gujarat. But this too did not lead to a federation in the strict sense, since each of these units had pre-existed and had no bilateral or multilateral agreements with one another.

Eventually, the States Reorganisation Act of 1956 took shape and changed the state boundaries in the country. Subsequently in later decades, as we know, new states were created—Jharkhand (from Bihar), Chhattisgarh (from Madhya Pradesh), Uttarakhand (from Uttar Pradesh) and Telangana (from Andhra Pradesh)—this time, to further the interests of effective administration.

THE DEBATE CONTINUES

I am an ardent follower of the Constitution of India, as established by law. I hold that there is no greater or higher road map for the country's governance than the Constitution. To me, the Constitution does not mean just a text drafted by the eminent jurist and Constitutional Adviser Sir B.N. Rau, and given to the president of the Constituent Assembly. Article 356 is also part of the Constitution. The constitutional position has not changed in this matter, although it may have undergone changes elsewhere; for instance, with respect to the 42nd Amendment and the 44th Amendment.

The 42nd Amendment was made in Indira Gandhi's tenure during the Emergency, and it sought to curtail the powers of the judiciary in the pronouncement of the constitutional validity of laws. It also laid down the fundamental duties of citizens. The 44th Amendment, which came during the Janata Party rule led by Morarji Desai, sought to nullify a number of provisions that had come by way of the 42nd Amendment and to restore the Constitution to its pre-1976 status. For instance, the new amendment protected the fundamental rights of citizens from being tampered with through legislations and through the use of Article 352. Even the grounds for the declaration of a national Emergency were changed; earlier it was external aggression and internal disturbances, but under the 44th Amendment, 'internal disturbances' was replaced with 'armed rebellion'.

My stand on Article 356 did not change, whether as an MP or as president. However, as president, I had the opportunity to examine it in detail because it is the president who issues the proclamation for the imposition of Article 356, which leads to the dismissal of a state government. When we talk of an emergency here, the reference is to the breakdown of government machinery in a state, in which the president, on the advice of the Union Council of Ministers, invokes Article 356 and President's Rule is imposed. According to Article 356:

(1) If the President, on receipt of a report from the Governor of a State or otherwise, is satisfied that a situation has arisen in which the Government of the State cannot be carried on in accordance with the provisions of this Constitution, the President may, by Proclamation—
   a. assume to himself all or any of the functions of the Government of the State and all or any of the powers vested in or exercisable by the Governor or anybody or authority in the State other than the Legislature of the State;

b. declare that the powers of the Legislature of the State shall be exercisable by or under the authority of Parliament;
c. make such incidental and consequential provisions as appear to the President to be necessary or desirable for giving effect to the objects of the Proclamation, including provisions for suspending in whole or in part the operation of any provisions of this Constitution relating to anybody or authority in the State:

Provided that nothing in this clause shall authorize the president to assume to himself any of the powers vested in or exercisable by a High Court, or to suspend in whole or in part the operation of any provision of this Constitution relating to High Courts.

When the Constitution was drafted, the state of Emergency as regards Article 356 was originally for six months. With the 42nd Amendment, it became three years and with the 44th Amendment it was brought down to one year. I remember that, when the 44th Amendment was introduced, it was passed in the Lok Sabha since there was no problem in getting two-thirds majority. Ratification by state legislatures could come later. In the original draft, it was proposed that the entire provision of Article 356 should be deleted. The Congress, to which I belonged then, however, opposed it in the Rajya Sabha. We managed enough numbers to pre-empt the move since its passage required two-thirds of the total numbers present and voting in both Houses of Parliament. We threatened to nip the proposal in the bud.

A compromise was then worked out, and the duration of the state of emergency for which President's Rule gets imposed was brought to one year from the three years in the 42nd Amendment.

We must not sit in value judgement but deal with the provision in a pragmatic way. I felt that there was need for such powers with the Centre to deal with extraordinary circumstances. This extraordinary scenario actually materialized in the 80s in Punjab. The Khalistan agitation had begun, Giani Zail Singh had moved to the Centre as president and Darbara Singh was the CM of the state. The agitation was gathering momentum. The Centre decided to intervene because the situation was getting out of hand and the state government had failed to handle the crisis. President's Rule was proclaimed, and after six months it was re-proclaimed for another six months. But what was to be done next was an issue. The Constitution was amended, specifically for Punjab, and not once but several times, because elections could only be held only in 1992, which brought Beant Singh's government to power with a stable majority. For nearly five years at a stretch—from June 1987 to February 1992—there was President's Rule in the state.

Similarly, a state legislature may pass resolutions seeking secession. This cannot be allowed. The union government is constitutionally obliged to protect the sovereignty and integrity of India. We opposed the abolition of Article 356 on the ground that we could be faced with a situation in the future where the need for the Union Government to intervene becomes essential in the country's larger good, because of the total chaos prevailing in a state. Of course, I strongly feel that the provision should not be used for political purposes, to inflict injuries on political parties, but only to serve constitutional necessities it is meant for, and applied judiciously. It must not become an instrument of the union government to punish state regimes that are inimical to it. There is an established constitutional process. The governor sends his (or her) report; the cabinet examines it and then forwards it to the president with its recommendations.

For decades, there has been a debate on the use and misuse of Article 356, and both sides have been charged with various political allegations. There have been many instances of imposition of President's Rule that became talking points. President's Rule was proclaimed in Kerala, which dislodged the communist government of E.M.S. Namboodiripad, barely two years after the 1957 elections. There had been many instances of unrest in the state over radical reforms, especially the Agrarian Relations Bill and the Education Bill, which the Namboodiripad government had brought, and which the Catholic Church considered as an encroachment on its rights and powers. The situation turned grim over the weeks as Kerala was plunged into violence and the state government responded strongly. The union government led by Nehru then moved to impose President's Rule in the state. It was the first time in independent India's history that Article 356 was invoked, and that too to dismiss a popularly elected government with a clear majority. On occasions, internal problems of the ruling party were sought to be resolved through the imposition of Article 356—in Uttar Pradesh and in Punjab, for instance. Then there were cases where the failure of state machinery led to the proclamation of President's Rule. I believe that Article 356 has, by and large, served the nation well and should continue.

ARUNACHAL PRADESH

As president, I faced situations where presidential proclamations arising out of Article 356 were issued. One of the instances was that of Arunachal Pradesh, which had several complications and led to the involvement of the Supreme Court. Congress leader Nabam Tuki was then the CM and his brother Nabam Rebia was the Assembly Speaker. J.P. Rajkhowa took charge as governor of the state in June 2015. In the first week of November, he issued a notification for the sixth assembly session to meet on 14 January 2016. That same month, Congress MLAs demanded the removal of the deputy speaker while BJP legislators sought the removal of the speaker. There was political turmoil in the state. The governor then ordered the advancement of the assembly session to 16 December 2015.

The speaker issued a notice disqualifying 14 of the 21 Congress MLAs who had rebelled, and the deputy speaker, in turn, quashed the disqualification. It was a free-for-all in Arunachal Pradesh. The speaker also decided that the sixth session would not commence on 16 December. The Tuki government locked the assembly premises. All these developments led to a constitutional crisis. The assembly then met first in a hotel and later in a club, and moved a no-confidence motion against the speaker. He was replaced with another speaker. At that point, neither was President's Rule imposed nor had it been recommended to me. By the time my advice was sought, the matter had reached the court, with many legal luminaries arguing the matter from the two contesting sides.

In January 2016, the High Court stayed the disqualification

of the rebel Congress MLAs, and the Supreme Court agreed to hear a plea of the dislodged speaker against his removal. A Constitution Bench was formed to hear the case, particularly the constitutional scope of the discretionary powers of the governor. By the end of the month, the cabinet recommended President's Rule and Tuki filed a fresh plea against it. President's Rule was lifted in February, followed by rebel Congress leader Kalikho Pul taking oath as CM. Eventually, in July 2016, the apex court termed the governor's decision unconstitutional and ordered the restoration of the Tuki government. Eventually, Tuki resigned ahead of the floor test because he realized he did not have the numbers.

To my mind, Tuki could have initially taken the position that he was the CM and agreed to the assembly session, which had been notified by the governor and proved his majority. He should have ignored the removal of the speaker. There would have been no crisis then. But when he did not, and the issue spiralled out of control, I gave my assent to the proclamation of President's Rule. That said, I must confess that I was unhappy with the governor's action. I have always maintained that the governor is not the ruler of a state; he acts on the aid and advice of the Council of Ministers. The governor does not even belong to the state, so how can he take on the mantle of a ruler!

I do not recall if I met Rajkhowa, or his representative, specifically on this issue, but on several occasions in my meetings with governors of states and my various speeches, I stressed on the role that they should play—always underlining that they must refrain from political activities and stick to the role the Constitution gives them.

During this crisis, the home minister met me and discussed the developments in the state. I cannot divulge the details of the discussion because it is privileged information; even the Supreme Court cannot direct me to disclose it. At some point though, I had expressed my displeasure to the home minister on the governor's conduct. Everybody wanted to wait for the Supreme Court's verdict. I was expecting, as others were, of some interim order, but when it did not come, I had to act. The verdict, when it came, indicted the governor on all counts, but Rajkhowa did not quit. I told the home minister that if the governor did not act, I would have to—in other words, ask the governor to quit. Before signing the presidential proclamation, I had consulted legal experts.

The floor of the House is the only ground to test the majority, or otherwise, of a government. It cannot be conducted in a hotel or a club house or any other place. This is where I feel Rajkhowa went wrong. The governor ought to have waited for a couple of months and allowed the trust or no-trust vote to take place on the floor of the House. The S.D. Sharma panel had, in 1980, clearly laid down that the test of a government's numerical strength can be done only in the assembly (or Parliament), and not in some private place.[1] Rajkhowa was no one to summon the House on his own, let alone decide the agenda of the session. The agenda is decided by the leader of the House.

A good example of the way the matter should be conducted is available in the Dharma Vira case of 1967. As governor of West Bengal, he received a letter from some 18 MLAs against

---

[1] Constituent Assembly Debates, Book No. 2, Volume No. VII, p. 43, Lok Sabha Secretariat

CM Ajoy Mukherjee. The governor then asked Mukherjee to prove his majority in the assembly. The CM responded that he would so in the next scheduled session. He pointed out that the Budget had been recently passed, which proved that he held the trust of the House. There would be no great harm, he argued, if the trust vote could be conducted during the next session of the House.

UTTARAKHAND

The other instance of Article 356 being imposed during my tenure as president was that of Uttarakhand. Here, it was not the governor's report but the recommendation of the union government on which I had to act. I accepted the recommendation of the home minister for imposition of President's Rule, because, according to the Constitution, the president has to act on the basis of the report of the governor of a state, or otherwise. The term 'otherwise' could mean any other relevant authority of the government. In the case at hand, it was the union home minister.

The crisis in Uttarakhand began in March 2016, when nine rebel Congress legislators (who had joined the BJP) demanded a vote on the Appropriation Bill, but the speaker claimed that the bill had been adopted by voice vote and adjourned the House. This led to a furore and, in the developing political uncertainty, the governor asked the then CM Harish Rawat to prove his majority on the floor of the assembly. Meanwhile, the speaker issued notices of disqualification to the rebel Congress MLAs. The High Court dismissed their plea for a stay on the show cause notices.

The PM, in New Delhi, presided over a cabinet meet and the Centre decided to recommend President's Rule. On 26 March 2016, at 11.15 pm, Arun Jaitley, the then union minister of finance and Nripendra Misra, principal secretary to the PM, met me in the study to brief me on this cabinet decision. At the outset, I told them that the government should wait for 36 hours before taking a decision. I made it clear that such decisions should be in keeping with the various judicial pronouncements on the subject, including that in the Dharam Vira and the S.R. Bommai cases.

However, I had no discretion in the case. I could have returned the file recommending President's Rule in the state, for reconsideration, but that would have served no purpose except to make headlines. I was clear that I did not want to add to the already brewing controversy. A day before Rawat was to prove his strength, President's Rule was imposed. As things turned out, Rawat was asked by the Supreme Court, where the matter had landed, to demonstrate his majority on the floor of the House. Had the government taken the points I had raised into consideration before deciding on President's Rule, it could have perhaps avoided the embarrassment of the High Court's *obiter dicta*.

The president's rights and authority are clearly defined in the Constitution. He can use his discretion and appoint a PM in case of a vacuum. For example, Giani Zail Singh appointed Rajiv Gandhi as PM soon after Indira Gandhi's assassination. He used his discretionary powers, because then there was no Council of Ministers on whose aid and advice he could act.

Article 74 is clear that the president acts in accordance

with the advice of the Council of Ministers: 'There shall be a Council of Ministers with the PM at the head to aid and advice the President who shall, in the exercise of his functions, act in accordance with such advice.' The phrase 'who shall…' was added by the Constitution (42nd) Amendment Act, 1976. Later on, the 44th amendment inserted the following: 'Provided that the President may require the Council of Ministers to reconsider such advice, either generally or otherwise, the President shall act in accordance with the advice tendered after such reconsideration.' It is clear from these provisions that the discretionary powers of the president are limited.

I accept that a number of governors, in seeking to invoke Article 356 or conducting themselves in times of political turmoil, have interfered in politics. And there have also been cases when the speaker, who should be non-partisan, threatened that he would act against the interests of the ruling government in case he is not made the CM. This happened in at least two instances in Manipur, and is indicative of the failure of the constitutional machinery.

The use of Article 356 has also been done to justify the Mandate Theory. A party that comes to power at the Centre with the people's mandate proceeds to dismissing state governments belonging to the opposition parties, on the ground that the same voters who had brought them to power in the states had expressed lack of faith in them, later in the Lok Sabha elections. The Janata Party government had, in 1977, dismissed state governments on this theory, and Indira Gandhi did the same when she returned to power in 1980. In the second case, I had a major argument with my then party leaders on a resolution that had been adopted to dismiss the non-Congress governments.

Article 356 is neutral, neither positive nor negative. If it can be misused, it has its legitimate uses too, like in the case of Punjab. I will always reiterate my support to the continuation of this provision in the Constitution.

CHAPTER 5

JUDICIARY, THE PILLAR OF DEMOCRACY: ITS REACH; ITS LIMITS

In a parliamentary democracy, which India is, there are three main state organs—the executive, the legislature and the judiciary. In the constitutional scheme of things, the first two are closely interlinked and have to often work together to ensure that parliamentary democracy functions unhindered. This has been more or less the case since the country adopted its Constitution, and any confrontation that emerges is resolved through established procedures and rules. The judiciary, though, is not part of this arrangement. It has been kept apart. Its task is to observe from a distance. Despite this, there emerges some friction among the executive, legislature and the judiciary, which is undesirable. It is the primary responsibility of the government of the day to avoid needless confrontations.

However, the judiciary too has a role to play here. It cannot live in an ivory tower and in isolation, because the judiciary is often called upon to pass judgements on decisions of the executive and the legislatures, whether the state assemblies or the Parliament. It has to study issues emanating from government decisions, which follow a set pattern—when a government decides on a policy or programme, the matter is placed before the Cabinet, and in every Cabinet note, the minister concerned indicates whether the matter had been approved by the Ministry of Finance, and the Ministry of Law and Justice, if required.

The constitutional framework clearly lays down the roles of the three pillars of democracy, and the framework desires that neither of them infringes on the jurisdiction of the other. The judiciary has no executive brief. The executive implements its own decisions, resolutions adopted by Parliament or state assemblies, as well as the rulings of the judiciary. A fine balance has to be maintained by all concerned, and this balance remains undisturbed so long as the basic principle—that neither of them will interfere in the powers of the other—is respected and adhered to.

However, the judiciary does have the power of interpretation. It can interpret laws framed by the legislature to ensure that they do not infringe upon the Constitution. In the name of interpretation, the courts cannot make new laws, because enacting laws is the sole prerogative of the legislature. To some extent, the judiciary can oversee the implementation of laws, but that is all. It is not the judiciary's job to pass judgements on legislative and executive decisions that have been adopted through a majority in Parliament unless these decisions alter the basic structure of the Constitution.

This constitutional division prevailed for decades since Independence and functioned smoothly. But in recent times, many believe that the judiciary has become hyperactive. I have referred to the popular phrase 'judicial activism' on several occasions. This refers to the conduct of judges overreaching their constitutional mandate. In several speeches and addresses to the judiciary, I have said that judges must always respect the constitutional division between the executive and the judiciary. The judiciary must refrain from stepping into the jurisdiction of either the executive or the Parliament. The final say is, and must remain, with the Parliament and the executive, and not with the judiciary. I believe it is essential to keep underlining this important division of powers, else there will be chaos.

Perhaps, the judiciary extends its mandate out of overenthusiasm. But it is still not justifiable, even though some people welcome it. In some countries, people initially welcomed military or dictatorial rule, as they were dejected with the current state of affairs. Military rulers were even felicitated by the public. However, over a period of time, people got to see the real face of such regimes and realized the dangers they had put themselves into. Similarly, judicial overreach may sound attractive in the early stages, but the long-term impact may not be conducive to parliamentary democracy. It is important to maintain constitutional propriety and not be overwhelmed by public opinion.

To an extent, the intervention of the judiciary may be a pointer to the deficiency of the executive in some matters. Still, whether buses will be run on CNG is something for the executive and not for the judiciary to decide, though the judiciary can involve itself in the larger act of protecting the environment. The judiciary has engaged itself in some excesses at times. A judge of the Calcutta High Court once held court in the midst of a traffic congestion, summoning police and traffic personnel! Another judge, seeking reservations, used a platform as a court! Limits of judicial reach cannot be crossed in this manner. There are rules and laws, both in writing and also implicit. Yet, I will not go to the extent of saying that the judiciary has become a superpower in itself.

There have been instances where judicial verdicts were difficult or even impossible to implement. If a judgement is hard to implement, nobody will execute it. Judges also often make observations that are recorded in a written order but are not necessarily part of the judgement. That is termed as *obiter dicta*. Such observations are not legally binding as a precedent or even in the case at hand. However, newspaper reports often give great publicity to these observations as if they are part of the legally binding judgement.

The judiciary is a responsible organ of democracy and it has a number of protections. The President (on the advice of the PM) can dissolve Parliament and call for fresh elections; people can vote a party out of power and get in a new party at the helm. But judges cannot be easily removed; the impeachment process to remove them is both stringent and long. Clearly, as people say, the judiciary must remain independent, but I maintain that the judiciary must always remain alert. People should have no doubts with regards to its integrity. After all, Caesar's wife must not only be above suspicion but also seen to be so. I am not talking of sentiments, but facts. There may be a popular perception on an issue, but that cannot be allowed to influence verdicts. Evidences and facts must form the basis of verdicts.

JUDICIAL APPOINTMENTS

In discussions on the judiciary, the process of appointing judges, especially to the Supreme Court and the High Courts, cannot be ignored. The system of selecting and appointing judges should be unquestionable. Here, we are faced with a peculiar situation, with a collegium comprising judges selecting fellow judges, and the government being accorded a mere confirmative role. This had not always been the case. Since 1950 and right until the early 90s, the process involved the executive appointing judges to the higher courts in consultation with the CJI. But in 1993, in what has come to be called the Second Judges case, the Supreme Court converted 'consultation' into 'confirmation' and stated that the CJI had the powers to appoint (and transfer), in consultation with two seniormost judges of the apex court. It also said that the 'role of the Chief Justice of India is primal in nature' and the 'executive cannot have an equal say in the matter'. The president merely approves the selection of judges. Of course, even otherwise, the president does not recommend names to the collegium, but acts on the aid and advice of the Council of Ministers. It is for the judiciary and the executive to resolve differences that arise on issues of appointment and transfer of judges.

The Second Judges verdict became a precursor to the collegium system that we have in place today. In October 2015, the apex court struck down the National Judicial Appointments Commission (NJAC) Act, 2014, through a 4:1 majority order, and the constitutional amendment that had paved the way for the establishment of the commission was declared 'unconstitutional and void'. The NJAC Act and the amendment had been passed by Parliament with support across the board. The commission would have consisted of six members—the CJI, the two seniormost judges of the Supreme Court, the union law minister and two 'eminent persons' to be nominated by a panel consisting of the PM, the leader of the Opposition and the CJI.

In declaring it void, the Supreme Court restored the collegium system that had operated before. The presiding judge on the five-judge Constitution Bench, Justice J.S. Khehar, said: 'It is difficult to hold that the wisdom of appointment of judges can be shared with the political-executive. In India, the organic development of civil society has not as yet sufficiently evolved.' The court also later dismissed a plea seeking a review of its order striking down the NJAC, saying that the review request had no merit and that there had been a long delay of 470 days in filing the plea for review.

I have serious doubts over the present arrangement, and the judiciary ought to relook into the issue. The country is run by a political system in which members, who sit in Parliament and assemblies, are elected by the people. They represent the collective will of the people, and nobody can ignore this reality. The pre-collegium system had existed for years since 1950, and there had been no major problems that necessitated a change. One argument that has been given in favour of the collegium system is that it can more effectively tackle the issue of a large number of vacancies in the higher judiciary. If that indeed is the case, then the proponents of the collegium system must tell the nation if the collegium has succeeded in that task. Besides, let us not forget that we have had some eminent judges under the old system, before the collegium came into being.

It is possible that the judiciary has come to mistrust the executive or the legislature and, therefore, does not want them to have decisive powers on the appointment of judges. It does not, in its own words, wish to be caught in a 'web of indebtedness' through the NJAC. This mistrust is not good for the healthy administration of the country and should be avoided. Better communication between the parties concerned can help in dispelling such mistrust.

Justice J. Chelameswar, former judge of the Supreme Court, had raised doubts over the collegium system. There have been others, even those who opposed the NJAC, who have been critical of the manner in which the collegium has worked in appointing judges. I don't want to comment specifically on any particular judge's opinion, because eventually, the majority view prevails in a court verdict. There have been several verdicts that have had a major impact on the people and the political system, and these rulings came with a wafer-thin majority. These include the much-discussed Golaknath and the Kesavananda Bharati cases. In the former, the apex court had, in 1967, by a slim majority of 6:5, held that Parliament could not tamper with the fundamental rights provisions in the Constitution. The majority view did not accept that Article 368 contained powers given to the executive or the legislature to amend, but that it merely laid down the procedure for amendment. Besides, since Article 13(2) prohibited the Parliament from making laws that abridged fundamental rights, Article 368 was an ordinary law within the ambit of Article 13(2). The five judges who held a minority view had argued that the law, as it stood, could not be prospectively overruled. They based their opinion on what is known as the Blackstonian theory, which holds that a law takes effect from the date of it coming into force and that this effect cannot be superseded through prospective overruling.

In the 1973 Kesavananda Bharati versus State of Kerala case, a 13-judge Constitution Bench, again with a thin majority of 7:6, gave back to Parliament the right to amend the Constitution provided its 'basic structure' was not altered. In his dissenting judgement, Justice H.R. Khanna said that while Parliament had the right to amend, it could not tinker with the basic structure of the Constitution.

The dissenting voices in these verdicts could not be ignored because they were in a substantial number. While the process lays down that the majority voice is supreme, the minority ruling cannot be simply brushed aside because it is also based on material facts, and the arguments put forth by the dissenting voice are used in taking decisions. For instance, Justice Khanna's minority verdict set the tone for what has come to be understood as the basic structure doctrine of the Constitution of India.

ACHIEVING BALANCE

People sometimes say that judges are an insulated lot and that they ought to be more sociable. In our democratic concept, I feel that judges, especially of the higher judiciary, do not generally interact with other stakeholders. A certain distance has to be maintained, given the judiciary's role in adjudicating various actions of the executive. However, there should be more frequent interactions between the executive and the judiciary. If the CJI were to meet the PM more regularly—and similarly the Chief Justice of High Courts were to interact with the respective CMs more often—a number of vexatious issues could be resolved, and the balance that is needed to be maintained between them can be achieved.

The loss of balance at times is a disturbing phenomenon. But this was not always the case. Prior to the 1991–93 verdicts of the apex court, there was a sense of balance between the executive and the judiciary and also between Parliament and the judiciary. But with the Supreme Court deciding that it would select and appoint judges to the higher judiciary, areas of confrontation emerged, causing disruption in the fine balance that has been provided for in the Constitution.

As president, I made attempts to interact with the judges. I would invite them over for tea and photo sessions. Unfortunately, there were not enough occasions to meet them otherwise. I would see them on formal occasions, including the swearing-in ceremony of the CJI. These welcome and farewell events were, of course, rare. I was sworn in by CJI Kapadia. Then I had the opportunity to host dinner for various others—Altamas Kabir, P. Sathasivam, R.M. Lodha, H.L. Dattu, T.S. Thakur and J.S. Khehar, among others.

A lot can be said about delays in the justice delivery system, but the courts too work under many constraints. There are not enough courtrooms and judges. The judicial infrastructure needs major expansion, which in turn requires funds. The expenditure on the judiciary comes under non-plan expenditure, and there have not been enough funds to spend in revamping the judicial infrastructure. The ratio of judges to the population is also worryingly low. According to the Ministry of Law and Justice, India has 20 judges per 10 lakh people; it faced a combined shortage of over 6,000 judges, including over 5,000 in the lower courts. As CJI Thakur had in 2016 told a gathering in the PM's presence, the 'entire burden' (of vacancies and the growing pending cases) could not be shifted onto the judiciary.

The crisis, however, is a complicated one and cannot be resolved through instant or populist methods. Besides, at times, neither the government nor the judiciary can do much. For instance, the tendency to litigate, although a democratic right, leads to problems. There are issues that can be resolved by other means. According to various reports, the government happens to be the biggest litigator in various courts.

In the face of this onslaught, what can be done? If the judiciary decides to shorten the process of litigation with intent to settle cases faster, there will be cries of protest from various quarters, with the allegation that the justice system is being short-circuited and made unfair. But the fact remains that vacancies have to be filled quickly. Take the Allahabad High Court, which has the highest number of sanctioned strength of judges among all High Courts; it has also had a high number of vacancies, although various attempts have been made to fill those vacancies.

The primary responsibility of filling these vacancies now lies with the collegium, a system that the Supreme Court has adopted after rejecting the NJAC. Incidentally, there is no provision in the Constitution of India for the establishment of a collegium to select judges to the apex court and the High Courts. But now that the system is in place, the members of the collegium have to ensure that the problem of vacancies is addressed effectively.

Inordinate delays in the appointment of judges also deny opportunities to the deserving. A judge who is appointed after his junior and thus takes oath later, goes up the seniority ladder, which could adversely affect his chances of promotion, either in the High Court or the Supreme Court. It is the responsibility of both the collegium and the government to avoid such fallacies.

In the final analysis, the Supreme Court has remained substantially balanced, with only a few aberrations here and there. Our judiciary has given relief to the people when they needed it the most. Nowhere in the world would you have instances where the courts take cognizance of grievances of the common man sent through a simple postcard, and provide justice.

CHAPTER 6

DEALING WITH MERCY PETITIONS: HUMANE AND LEGAL ASPECTS

As president, I dealt with several matters that were both complicated and taxing. But none caused me as much pain or anguish as the task of deciding on mercy petitions filed before me by convicts sentenced to death. The death sentences emanated from judgements of a trial court, later upheld by a High Court and finally by the Supreme Court. The trial court's verdict would be based on facts as the judge saw it, and the High Court's ruling would take the point of law into consideration. The apex court considered the case in an overall perspective before giving its verdict. Once these legal avenues are exhausted, the convict approaches the president for commutation of the capital punishment.

The president is not the punishing authority; the punishment has already been given by the courts. The president is the last resort. Thus, a humane aspect arises by the time the president comes into the picture. I was constantly aware while handling such cases that I was the last hope for the convict and that his life was in my hands. It was not an ordinary, routine government file that I was dealing with. I used to take more than a week to read the case history and the court judgements. But I took no more than three weeks in all to dispose off a file.

During my tenure as president, I rejected 30 mercy pleas involving nearly 40 convicts. My distinguished predecessors, A.P.J. Abdul Kalam and Pratibha Patil, had left a large number of cases pending. In fact, Kalam hardly disposed off any mercy pleas while Patil had decided on a few of them. The latter had granted clemency to 34 convicts and rejected just three petitions for mercy. Different presidents have different approaches.

I saw no point in keeping such files pending. The ones I dealt with dated as far back as the years 2000, 2004, 2005 and 2007. Either way, they had to be decided and I took it upon myself to discharge the responsibility. The law of the land had to be upheld. While I deliberated long and hard over the files of mercy pleas, once I had taken a decision—even of rejecting them—I let the issue rest. I may have had sleepless nights while considering my decision, but after the decision was made, the matter was closed as far as I was concerned. I did not follow the developments thereafter in detail, though I did keep in touch with the issue in the general sense. It is a futile exercise for a president to closely follow the trajectory after he has done his job. I cannot say for certain if my successors will follow my example of disposing of mercy petitions quickly; after all, I did not follow the example of my predecessors.

On its part, the Supreme Court itself had stayed the execution of convicts in a number of cases on the ground that these cases were pending for years. The court's argument was that if the cases were nine years or older, the convicts given the death sentence had suffered all these years and their pain must be taken into consideration. Obviously, these cases never came to me for consideration. There were also cases where the government moved an appeal, and I told the government to get the court's position through the Attorney General of India. Though the then Home Minister Sushil Kumar Shinde had forwarded a large number of cases, recommending death penalty, many of these were held back due to the court's intervention.

Over the years, broad outlines for dealing with mercy petitions had evolved. However, three factors played on my mind. The first factor was that the case by nature must have involved ferocity and cruelty, and it must fall within the rarest of rare category. Two, the death sentence, given by the trial court, should have been upheld by the High Court and the Supreme Court without any dissenting voice—in other words, with unanimous verdicts. And three, the Government should have recommended the rejection of the petition. Once these conditions were met, the president ought to have no problems in setting aside the mercy petition. This is the position I took as president. Generally, once the president rejects a mercy plea, the matter does not return to the Supreme Court unless fresh issues of technicality or legality are introduced. In certain cases, appeals for mercy are made to the governor. I do not recollect any instance where I granted mercy after the governor had rejected the plea.

I would carefully read through the details, and even the court proceedings and verdicts, if they were in English. If they were in Hindi or a local language, then I would seek to understand the gist of the issue. In most cases, the judgements were in English. I remember a case that I read in detail, where a daughter (in collaboration with her husband) had killed her father and younger brothers over a property issue. The Sessions Court's ruling was in Hindi.

Several mercy pleas, including that of Ajmal Kasab, one of the executioners of the 26/11 Mumbai massacre, were of high-profile nature and attracted a great deal of attention. I was shocked that a man of such tender age had adopted the path of large-scale violence. He knew he would be hanged if caught, and yet he conducted the terror attack. People like him get misled because of the training and brainwashing they receive from their handlers. But none of these factors affected my decision-making, which was based purely on the facts of the terror attack. Here was a man who had been convicted by the trial court, and the conviction had been upheld by the High Court and the Supreme Court unanimously. He had crossed over from Pakistan, though Pakistan officially denied it and even disowned him as a Pakistani. His mother was in Pakistan but even she did not come forward to acknowledge her son's identity. I told the then Pakistani president, Asif Ali Zardari, that Kasab could not have come from some other planet; all evidence pointed to him being a Pakistani. Could Zardari deny that Karachi was in Pakistan?

Kasab's mercy plea had been kept pending by my predecessor, and thus there had been a delay in deciding on it. I was not aware of the time and date of his hanging beforehand. Files moved in New Delhi and the execution was carried out in Mumbai. It was not necessary for me to be kept informed. There are norms and procedures to be followed in such cases and I suppose they were adhered to. As far as I was concerned, my role ended once I rejected his mercy plea.

The other instances were that of Afzal Guru and Yakub Memon. In the former case, the BJP was in the Opposition then and demanded Afzal's hanging without further delay. His mercy plea had not originally come to me. It had been placed before my predecessor who kept it pending, and thus there had been a delay in deciding on it. He had been convicted for his role in the 2001 attack on Parliament, and was hanged in February 2013 after I rejected his mercy plea. There was a great deal of hue and cry over the episode, with certain rights groups claiming that he had not been given adequate legal representation and that his execution was carried out in secrecy. Amnesty International had said the execution pointed to a 'worrying and regressive trend towards executions shrouded in secrecy'. There were Leftists and some activists from Jawaharlal Nehru University (JNU) that campaigned against his death sentence.

The case itself went through many phases. He was arrested by a Special Cell of the Delhi Police in December 2001 and charged under various provisions of the Indian Penal Code (IPC) and later the Prevention of Terrorism Act, 2002 (POTA). The court-appointed lawyer for the accused later withdrew from the case, citing overload of work, and another lawyer was appointed. A few others, including former Delhi University professor, S.A.R. Geelani, were also arrested in connection with the case and tried.

Afzal made a confessional statement that was recorded by the appropriate authority of Delhi Police, but his lawyer subsequently alleged that the confession had been extracted from his client under duress. Afzal too disowned that confession, which was thereafter not taken by the court as evidence against him. Trial continued in a special court and concluded in six months following a day-to-day hearing. Afzal was given capital punishment, and so was Geelani. The matter went to the Delhi High Court, which upheld Afzal's sentence but acquitted Geelani. The Supreme Court too upheld the death penalty, and later on dismissed a review petition filed by Afzal. The convicted terrorist then filed a mercy plea before me.

In November 2012, I had sent seven cases, including Afzal Guru's, back to the Ministry of Home Affairs. I requested the then Home Minister, Sushil Kumar Shinde, to review the opinion of his predecessor P. Chidambaram. A couple of months later, the home minister made his final recommendation, seeking the death penalty. I then rejected the mercy plea and Afzal was hanged in February 2013.

Yakub Memon's case was equally controversial. He was executed in July 2015. He had been convicted and given death sentence by a special Terrorist and Disruptive Activities (Prevention) Act court in 2007 in the 1993 Mumbai bomb blasts case. The court found that he was part of a criminal conspiracy to conduct terrorist attacks, disruptive activities and murder. Besides, he was charged with illegal possession of arms and ammunition. Memon's appeal before the Supreme Court did not succeed, as the court confirmed the capital punishment he had been awarded, saying that he was the 'mastermind' and 'driving force' behind the terror bombings. The court also rejected a review plea he filed later. His mercy plea file came to me thereafter. Taking everything into consideration, I rejected his request in July 2015. My decision came in the wake of a detailed discussion I had with the then home minister, Rajnath Singh, and the then solicitor general, Ranjit Kumar. But the matter did not end there. Memon filed a writ with the Supreme Court, saying that the execution be stayed till his mercy plea with the governor was decided—the Maharashtra governor had been petitioned too. I was flooded with letters from certain eminent personalities and political leaders, requesting me to reconsider my decision.

The convicted person had also filed a writ petition before the apex court, this time challenging the order passed in a curative petition he had moved, claiming that the required quorum was not present, based on the interpretation of the rules of the Supreme Court. The two judges hearing the matter thereafter requested the CJI to urgently constitute a larger Bench and settle the matter. But Memon failed to get any relief even there. Finally, as a last resort, his lawyers filed a fresh plea for a 14-day relief in the execution of the order on the ground that the president's consideration of the mercy plea was too close to the execution date, thus giving an impression that the president may not have had sufficient time to apply his mind. The court met at midnight and in the early hours of the day, upheld the execution. He was hanged in Nagpur jail. Memon had claimed innocence all through the trial.

Unlike in Kasab's case, where I had no doubts whatsoever, in the other two cases discussed above I was careful because of the various shades of opinion from both, those who wanted Memon and Afzal to be hanged and those who opposed the capital punishment. While I, as president, had applied my mind to all the cases of mercy pleas that were presented to me with recommendations of the government, the fact remains that the president normally goes by the recommendations of the Ministry of Home Affairs in such cases. If the government recommends the rejection of a mercy plea, then the president has to concur; if the government favours a mercy petition being accepted, the president does so. I believe that if the government of the day recommends that a mercy plea should be rejected, then I as president must not stand in the way.

However, there was one important case in which I did accept the mercy petition. It was in the infamous Bara massacre. In February 1992, armed men allegedly belonging to the Maoist Communist Centre—now named the Communist Party of India (Maoist)—brutally killed nearly three dozen villagers of the upper-caste Bhumihar community in Bara village in Gaya, Bihar. The victims were herded on the banks of a nearby canal, their hands tied and their throats slit. Some 36 people were accused of the crime, but charges were framed against 13. A Sessions Court convicted nine of them and gave death sentences to four in 2001. The capital punishment was confirmed by the Supreme Court in 2002. Their mercy pleas came to me for consideration.

The issue was a matter concerning Dalits and the massacre was some sort of retaliation on the atrocities committed on members of this community by other people. I recall having gone through the case in great detail, reading the court proceedings and the judgements. The Bara case had left a deep emotional impact on me, but I took the view—as I did in other cases—that my personal sentiments must not cloud the fact that in decision-making, the actions and functions of the state machinery should be taken into consideration. I granted mercy and commuted the death sentence of the four Bara massacre convicts because I found that the killers had acted in an exceptional frame of mind—even the court had made a similar observation. One of the convicts was very young, and courts usually take into consideration the age factor in deciding on capital punishment.

Normally, the established process is that, once the execution of a convict is decided upon, after all legal avenues have been exhausted by the convict and his family, then the convict's relatives should be informed of the date and time of the execution. If family members—wife or children, for example—wish to visit the convict one last time, that too is facilitated. These formalities were not possible in Kasab's case since nobody from Pakistan came forward with such requests. Our High Commission in Islamabad tried to contact the family members, but Pakistan's attitude was non-cooperative. We also did not hear from Kasab's mother. However, in the cases of Yakub Memon and Afzal Guru, perhaps these formalities were not fully adhered to.

It is possible that in certain cases, pressure can be brought upon by the media, etc., to change the course of justice. In the celebrated Nanavati case of the 1950s, for instance, public opinion was strongly and largely in favour of the accused, Commander K.M. Nanavati, then a serving officer of the Indian Navy, who had killed his wife's lover. We had the jury system then, and the jury held him not guilty of culpable homicide, deciding instead that he had shot the victim in the heat of the moment—it was a crime of passion. But the Bombay High Court dismissed the jury's arguments and ordered a retrial, in which the High Court found him guilty of culpable homicide. As a result of public support and strong backing from a section of the media, Nanavati was granted a presidential pardon after he had spent three years behind bars. Incidentally, the case saw the end of the jury system in India.

ABOLITION OF CAPITAL PUNISHMENT

The cases of mercy petitions and the courts granting death sentence have led to some people demanding the abolition of capital punishment. More recently, the issue had come up in the Memon and Guru cases. I am not very enamoured by the popular sentiment that the death penalty should be scrapped. Deterrence is absolutely needed in the rarest of rare cases. We must leave it for the judge to decide which case falls in the rarest of rare category, demanding capital punishment. Questions have been raised on the deterrence as well on the humane factors.

Already, the matter has been taken up at various levels. In August 2015, the Law Commission of India had submitted a report to the government, recommending that death penalty should be abolished except in cases relating to terrorism or crimes of waging war against the nation. This is in contrast to a wide range of crimes that are listed in the IPC that are considered appropriate for the death sentence. In both 2007 and 2012, India had voted against resolutions in the United Nations (UN) that called for a moratorium on capital punishment. It is clear that various experts, legal and constitutional, believe that the death penalty must remain, though only to be strictly used in the rarest of rare instances.

Besides, let us not forget that death sentences have been commuted to life term in cases where the judiciary felt inordinate delays had been caused in the legal process. In early 2014, the

Supreme Court had commuted the sentence of 15 death row convicts. It said that delays ranging from seven to 11 years in the disposal of mercy pleas could be grounds for clemency. Former PM Rajiv Gandhi's killers escaped from the death penalty on the ground that there had been a decade-long delay in disposing of their mercy petitions. The court also established a guideline, among others, wherein a 14-day gap was set up between the rejection of a mercy plea and the actual execution. The Centre, however, has approached the Supreme Court to introduce a 7-day deadline for death row convicts to file mercy petitions.

There should be an informed debate on the subject and the public must know the advantages and disadvantages of capital punishment. It is not an electoral issue to be contested by political parties. Legal experts, constitutional experts and civil rights activists must discuss it. But, for now, capital punishment is there in the IPC, drafted by the British some 150 years ago, and no purpose is served by having political debates on the subject.

CHAPTER 7

FOREIGN POLICY: MAINTAINING BALANCE; USING LEVERAGE

India's foreign policy has been one of continuity with change over the decades. It has evolved alongside global developments—the Cold War era, the post-Cold War period, the end of the bipolar superpower system, the emergence of China and the growing influence of India on the international platform. I served as external affairs minister under two PMs, Narasimha Rao and Dr Manmohan Singh, and the continuity remained irrespective of the minor changes that individual PMs gave to the country's foreign policy. Merely due to a change in government at the Centre, the country's foreign policy does not alter overnight.

There are certain core issues on which New Delhi's position has not changed despite the new emerging world order. For instance, India does not believe in being bracketed in one 'camp' or the other, while at the same time it has developed excellent relations with the major powers. Its relations with the US are cordial, even if there exist differences on matters of trade and visas. New Delhi's relationship with Russia remains as strong as it was in the early decades of Independence. It has a stable and working relationship with China despite the two countries having differences over borders and Beijing's support to Pakistan. India has, over the years, also established closer ties with Southeast Asian countries and the African continent. Besides, New Delhi has energized its cooperation with the immediate neighbours. Despite all of these endeavours, India's efforts to have better relations with Pakistan have consistently hit roadblocks.

And yet, I would not call Pakistan an 'enemy country', because no country is an enemy unless we are at war with it. We have diplomatic ties with Pakistan; both countries have their respective High Commissions on each other's soil, which are fully functional. Sometimes, a frail country that is not friendly is used to whip up strong sentiments in the domestic arena.

When Narendra Modi took over as PM, he had absolutely no experience in foreign affairs. As the CM of Gujarat, he had visited some countries, but those visits were limited to engaging for the good of his state, and had little to do with domestic or global foreign policies. Foreign policy was, therefore, a truly uncharted territory for him. But he did what no PM had attempted before: invite the heads of government/state of SAARC nations to his oath-taking ceremony in 2014—and this included Pakistan's then PM, Nawaz Sharif. His out-of-the-box initiative took several foreign policy veterans by surprise. As PM-designate, when Modi informed me of his decision, while the date of the oath-taking ceremony was fixed for 26 May 2014, I welcomed the move and advised him to ensure that all necessary security arrangements were in place for the high-profile foreign dignitaries who would visit the country on the occasion. It was a peculiar situation: the outgoing PM, Dr Singh, had tendered his resignation, which was accepted, and he had been asked to continue in office till the new government took over. As president, I discussed the matter of foolproof security with the agencies concerned. It was a challenge: the oath-taking ceremony was to be held outdoors and nearly 5,000 guests were expected to attend. Security was, therefore, considerably strengthened, apart from the issuance of a general alertness that is sounded for such events. I was relieved that everything went off smoothly.

I hosted dinner for the visiting dignitaries—some presidents, other PMs and one speaker of his country's national Parliament—at Rashtrapati Bhavan, which was attended by the PM and a few senior ministers of the new government (the portfolios were yet to be announced). I felt that the new PM's gesture of inviting the neighbouring countries was a good one, and that if we could keep this momentum, we would have vastly improved ties with our neighbours.

It was evident that one could expect the unexpected from Modi, because he had come with no ideological foreign policy baggage. He was to continue with these surprises: he made a sudden and unscheduled stop at Lahore in December 2015 to greet his then Pakistani counterpart, Nawaz Sharif, on the latter's birthday; and he initiated an annual informal summit with the Chinese president—one was held at Wuhan in China in 2018 and the other, more recently, at Mamallapuram in Tamil Nadu in 2019. I personally feel that PM Modi's stopover in Lahore was unnecessary and uncalled for, given the conditions that prevailed in India–Pakistan relations.

DEALING WITH PAKISTAN

Both India and Pakistan were born virtually the same day in August 1947. Within a decade of its existence, Pakistan came under military rule. The country slipped into political instability—seven PMs in 11 years, no general election and no worthwhile Constitution drafted by its Constituent Assembly for nine long years. As a result of these developments, a structured civilian government never gathered enough strength to stand firm and meet the challenge that the armed forces posed to democratic rule. The situation in India was vastly different. The Constitution was drafted within three years of its independence, and operationalized on 26 January 1950. The first general elections were held within five years of independence, in 1952; and the second in 1957, both for a union government and the states. Thereafter, the democratic system in India has grown stronger with time, with the armed forces playing the role they should in a parliamentary form of democracy.

One of the main difficulties that India has faced in building cordial ties with Pakistan is that the latter continues to hold negative thoughts. Since its inception, it has nurtured the belief that it did not receive its due at the time of Partition, and thus it has to make up for the loss by pursuing a policy of aggression against its bigger neighbour, India. Though it always held that it was equal or even superior to India, the fact is that Pakistan has lagged behind in every respect over the decades. The so-called equality concept and the dream to complete, by force, the supposedly unfinished agenda of Partition, has led Pakistan to depend on its armed forces to gain what it considers its legitimate claims.

Since 1947, Pakistan has engaged India through armed conflicts. In 1947, it organized a tribal invasion into the Kashmir valley, compelling India to push back the invaders, and finally accepting the UN's directive to stop at a line, which is now described as the Line of Control (LoC). Again, in 1965, Pakistan tried to capture Kashmir by armed intervention, but failed. The issue was brought to a close through the Soviet Union's intervention, with the Tashkent Declaration signed between Pakistan's military ruler General Ayub Khan and India's PM Lal Bahadur Shastri. But Pakistan's military adventures did not end there. Its ever-increasing dependence on its armed forces led to the 1971 war, which ended with the Pakistani forces having to accept a humiliating defeat and signing the instrument of surrender. The end of the war also led to the creation of a new nation, Bangladesh, with the division of Pakistan.

The defeat brought in a civilian government under the leadership of Zulfikar Ali Bhutto, first as president and then as PM of Pakistan. During his reign, Pakistan's Parliament approved a new Constitution by which he assumed office as PM and appointed a president. But the Pakistan Army did not take the development lying down. It unseated Bhutto through a military coup in July 1977. Under orders of General Zia-ul-Haq, Bhutto was arrested along with some members of his Cabinet, martial law was proclaimed and Zia-ul-Haq assumed power. Bhutto was released for a brief while, but rearrested. A trial took place, which many believed was unfair, and Bhutto was found guilty and given capital punishment. He was hanged in April 1979. The Army rule continued for a decade, but the military finally had to concede power to the democratic forces elected by the people. Though not well-structured or disciplined, democracy began to at least function in Pakistan.

Over the years, attempts by civilian governments to assert their authority over military dictates resulted in another phenomenon: the rise of religious fundamentalism. Today, terrorism fostered by the religious fundamentalists has begun to boomerang on the Pakistan government, which had used these fundamentalists to further their political objectives.

The established and accepted norm of conducting international relations is that it must happen between and among recognized governments. The armed forces is a part of the government in every country, but in a civilian government system these forces work under the command and authority of the elected civilian authorities. Pakistan has a unique setup, where the Army plays a major role in the country's decision-making, especially in policies relating to India. New Delhi cannot alter this situation, nor can it directly involve the Army into negotiations since there is a civilian democratic government in Pakistan. It is unfortunate that since Pakistan's formation, its statecraft has been dominated by the military, which has not been friendly to the Indian state, though India has made all efforts to reach out to Pakistan on numerous occasions in the past. For instance, after the terrorist attack on a military base in Pathankot in early 2016, India granted permission to a Joint Intelligence Team (JIT) from Pakistan to visit the place and conduct its own inquiries into the attack. This was because

New Delhi believed that the attack was planned from Pakistani soil and that the attackers had crossed over to India from Pakistan. In the given circumstances, the Indian government's decision was not wrong. The modality of the fact-finding visit and the access the Pakistani team was to be provided were matters for the government to decide, keeping the Indian security concerns in mind. The decision, per se, did not reflect on the maturity or lack of it in our foreign policy perceptions.

The issue of Pakistan and India's relations with its neighbour does come up during discussions the president or the PM has with other heads of state or government, here in India and abroad. On my visit to Belgium as president, I discussed the subject with the king and members of the government. There is nothing wrong in deliberating on such matters with foreign dignitaries, as it does not violate any standard protocol. Such discussions happen during bilateral talks or round table conferences also. I, thus, believe that I had committed no impropriety in criticizing Pakistan on foreign soil for its failure to take necessary action against anti-India activities.

Imran Khan's emergence as PM in August 2018 is an interesting development. So far, he has had the support of the Army of his country. But the Army's dominance in the affairs of Pakistan is nothing new. After 1956, when Pakistan came under military rule, there have been several civilian regimes that were supported by the Army; they also collapsed after the Army withdrew its patronage, leading to long spells of military rule. Besides, Ayub Khan, Yahya Khan and Zia-ul-Haq, there was General Pervez Musharraf, who overthrew the civilian government of Nawaz Sharif.

After Imran became the PM, some experts believed that there would be a shift in Islamabad's policy of encouraging cross-border terrorism into India. But that did not happen. India has, for long, been complaining that Pakistan indulges in fomenting terrorism on Indian soil through patronage to terrorist outfits operating from within Pakistan, including from Pakistan-occupied Kashmir (PoK). India has, on numerous occasions, furnished to the Pakistani authorities details of these terror operations, including the names of terrorists, terror outfits and the shelters they were provided in areas under Pakistani control. We have also reminded Pakistan repeatedly of the solemn assurance it gave to PM Vajpayee, that Pakistan would not allow its territory to be used by forces that are inimical to India. Though the indications so far from Pakistan under Imran's leadership have not been very encouraging, it is too early to arrive at a conclusion. We have to wait and see how the Pakistani PM proceeds with his foreign policy initiatives, especially with regard to India. His Foreign Minister, Shah Mahmood Qureshi, is an old hand; he had held the same portfolio in the Pakistan People's Party government in 2008, when the 26/11 terror attacks took place.

Though we have to wait and watch how Imran evolves, particularly with respect to issues concerning India, I personally feel that India must engage with him. He is part of a new breed of politicians, is born in the post-Independence period and does not carry the old baggage of pre-partition politics that the Muslim League personified. As the old saying goes, 'You can choose your friends but not your neighbours'.

India must pursue its Pakistan-related policies with utmost care and deft handling, and not through romanticizing its political approach. History shows that India has responded effectively to the challenge both militarily and diplomatically, depending upon the situation. Surgical strikes conducted by Indian forces across the border have been normal military operations in response to Pakistan's continued aggression. But there is really no need to over-publicize them—something that has been done ever since the Indian military conducted two strikes inside Pakistani territory since 2016. We gained nothing by over-talking on these operations.

STRENGTHENING INDIA–US TIES

Our relationship with the US has dramatically improved over the years. But to some extent, the bilateral ties have been at times shadowed by the American attitude of looking through the Pakistan prism. The US failed to understand the psyche of Pakistan—its burning desire to be treated as equal to India in all respects. The US pampered Pakistan merely to gain some strategic advantage, sometimes in its conflict with Russia (earlier the Soviet Union) or in its fight against the Taliban. The logistic advantages provided by Pakistan have blurred the US's vision about India's position in these matters. Pakistan may have been created out of India by the British and it is today a sovereign nation, but that does not erase the common cultural, ethnic and linguistic heritage the two countries share. The US's approach was exposed to the entire world during the liberation movement of Bangladesh, which ended in the India–Pakistan war of 1971.

The other example of Washington's jaundiced view was its refusal to accept the reality of terrorist attacks on India originating from Pakistani soil, and the complicity of Pakistan in those attacks. The US simply did not take India's position on these matters seriously enough. It took the twin attacks by terrorists on the World Trade Centre in New York and the Pentagon on 11 September 2001 for the US to be convinced that Pakistan was harbouring terrorists by giving them shelter, logistical support, training, etc. on its soil.

Historically speaking, the main conflict between the interests of the US and India arose from the aggressive American policies, particularly towards the upsurge of aspiration of the masses in different South Asian countries such as South Korea and the support to Chiang Kai-shek to the hilt against the People's Liberation Army (PLA) of China under Mao Zedong.

The other thorn in the India–US ties was India's decision to base its economic policies on a strong public sector foundation in the aftermath of independence. The role of free enterprise was constricted in India's economic development. Nehru, Indira Gandhi and all other Congress PMs until 1991 firmly subscribed to the view that the public sector should be the engine of economic growth. The US was for a free market and free enterprise, and, therefore, the difference was an ideological one.

The third area of difference was New Delhi's opposition to the restraints placed by the Treaty on the Non-Proliferation of Nuclear Weapons, or Non-Proliferation Treaty (NPT), and the Comprehensive Nuclear-Test-Ban Treaty (CTBT). While India favoured nuclear non-proliferation and a total ban on nuclear weapons programmes, it considered both the CTBT and the NPT as flawed, because they were discriminatory in nature and had created two groups—the nuclear-haves and the nuclear-have-nots.

Coincidentally, the five countries that fell in the first category were all permanent members of the UN Security Council (UNSC).

However, the last two areas of difference mentioned earlier evaporated with the post-1991 economic reforms undertaken during Narasimha Rao's prime ministership (with Dr Singh as the finance minister), and the signing of a civil nuclear agreement with the US in 2008. The agreement convinced the US of India's intention to pursue its nuclear programme for peaceful ends and New Delhi's affirmation of its non-proliferation approach.

Incidentally, it is not as if the US had not assisted India in the past, even during the Cold War era. New Delhi had received huge support from the US in its industrialization and agricultural programmes, through PL 480, a Food for Peace initiative. It led to the US helping out India in tackling foodgrains shortage in the 60s. But India never subscribed to the philosophy behind the Marshall Plan—an unwritten code that the recipient countries would extend their support to the US policy of containing the spread of communism.

Until the 90s, the India–US cooperation was confined to industry and technology, to some extent. It did not extend to the areas of defence and security. But with the end of the Cold War and the collapse of the Soviet Union in the late 80s, India had to look to Western markets for its military hardware requirements. As defence minister from 2004 to 2006, I had intensive discussions with the US Secretary of Defence, Donald Rumsfeld, both when he came to India and when I went to the US on a reciprocal visit. We signed a New Framework for the US-India Defense Relationship for the first time in 2005, which facilitated mutual cooperation in defence and security. Opposition to the agreement also came from traditional Congressmen, apart from the Left and the Right. Yashwant Sinha from the BJP questioned me about the definition of Framework Agreement by saying that it was nothing but a defence deal. And the communist parties made it far more ugly for me by getting into personal criticism. However, I faced Parliament single-handedly, and in hindsight it can be said with some degree of satisfaction that I won the debate.

Today, the US is one of India's major suppliers of military hardware and cutting-edge technology. In the area of security, our relationship is one of mutual dependence. Both countries favour uninterrupted trade flow through the international sea route, making it free from piracy and also from the extremist nationalistic approach of a littoral state.

As such, there are now no major areas of conflict in the India–US bilateral relations. Today, both are cooperating on a wide range of areas, such as terrorism and climate change. The India–US relationship is unfolding in its various facets, with the initial teething problems of the US's lack of appreciation of India's concerns now gradually being removed.

It is often remarked that the US is an unreliable power and India is a reluctant partner. I would say that the US, like any other country, particularly as a great power, has its own way of looking at things; it may not agree with the view of others. In international relations, every country tries to protect and further its national interests, and the US is no exception. Reliability is a relative term and should be analyzed in the context of the situation in which it is referred to. It is also tested on circumstances.

There is no doubt that PM Modi has made efforts to further improve the relationship between India and the US. He was the first PM of India to invite then US president, Barack Obama, as chief guest at the Republic Day parade in 2015. We had fruitful and productive discussions with Obama during his visit. Thereafter, in 2018, President Donald Trump was sounded out for the event, but this was formally turned down. The acceptance or rejection of an invite depends on the convenience of the guest, and nothing more should be read into it.

A great deal has been discussed on the impact of India–US relations with Trump becoming president in 2016. But a change of president does not necessarily significantly alter the policies of the US towards other countries, including India. As I mentioned earlier, the US had, under various presidents, supported Pakistan, and this continued until the tragic 9/11 incident. Thereafter, the US administration under different presidents took note of Pakistan's approach towards acts of terrorism, issued stern warnings and even, more recently, imposed cuts on military aid. Other countries, too, have begun to acknowledge Pakistan's role. As a result, Pakistan was placed on the watch-list of the Financial Action Task Force (FATF).

A lot has also been said about India's efforts at managing the dilemma of the India–US–China triangle in bilateral relations. The fact is that India–US ties and India–China relations are independent of each other. Since 1949, when the People's Republic of China (PRC) came to exist, the US refused to recognize it as the legitimate successor state in the mainland of China. It supported Chiang Kai-shek till the end, when he had lost control over mainland China and taken refuge in Formosa, now Taipei. From then on till 1971, the PRC was deprived of its legitimate seat as a permanent member in the UNSC. On its part, China termed the US as an aggressor in Korea and Vietnam. But that is now past; the US–China relationship has expanded multifold in areas of trade, industry and elsewhere. In fact, today, China's fast-growing economy poses a challenge to the US. American firms have invested hugely in China, and the transfer of technology has turned China into a substantial global economic force.

INDIA–CHINA PARTNERSHIP

India had, right from the start, recognized the ground reality in China. It was one of the first countries outside the Soviet Bloc to recognize and establish diplomatic relations with the PRC in 1949. And yet, despite having cordial ties with China, New Delhi did not hesitate to offer asylum to the Dalai Lama after Tibet was annexed by China and made into an autonomous region within the PRC. We also made it clear to China that India recognized Tibet as an integral part of the PRC and that the Dalai Lama was not in India to conduct any political activity. India also does not recognize the Tibetan government-in-exile and considers Dharamshala in Himachal Pradesh as the Dalai Lama's spiritual headquarters. The government had also not officially participated in an event to commemorate the 60th year of arrival of the Dalai Lama to India, apprehending that the event could be political in nature and draw China's ire.

At the Shangrila Dialogue organized in Singapore by the International Institute for Strategic Studies in 2018, PM Modi had remarked that 'Asia and the world will have a better future when India and China work together in trust and confidence.'

Years ago, Chinese President Hu Jintao had, while addressing a meeting organized by the Indian Council for Cultural Relations (ICCR), said he wanted the world to note that India and China had come together. However, both trust and confidence are not a certainty in the India–China relationship. It has had several ups and downs.

During these long years, our bilateral trade, since the early 90s, has grown manyfold. We have signed an agreement to maintain peace and tranquility along the Line of Actual Control in the border areas, and that agreement has substantially held. While the basic border issues between the two nations have not been resolved yet, several rounds of talks have taken place between the special representatives of both sides. The continuation of this dialogue is essential to resolving the border dispute.

In international relations, it is not possible for two nations to always be in agreement on all issues. There may be a common approach to some matters but differences in others. For instance, China has a definite view on the need for reforms in the UNSC, and India is not in agreement with that view—as well as with the views of a few other countries on the issue. We have our own viewpoint on what needs to be done to reform the system. China agreed to a one-time waiver to India on entering the Nuclear Suppliers Group (NSG), but it has opposed a permanent membership for India to this group.

Be that as it may, my view is that we cannot ignore China's stature as a mighty neighbour, and the fact that both India and China are ancient civilizations and share civilizational values as well. At the same time, India has to protect its national interests in dealing with China and keeping in mind the existing geopolitical situation in our neighbourhood. For example, India is vehemently opposed to China's Belt and Road Initiative (BRI) as it encroaches upon its sovereign rights (part of the project runs through PoK, which we consider as part of India but occupied by Pakistan). The construction of any road or high-level infrastructure in PoK is an infringement on India's sovereignty as India has always maintained that the entire undivided Jammu & Kashmir (J&K) is an integral part of this country.

There are also issues of bilateral trade that are essentially 'mono-commodity'. One of the biggest items of Indian export to China, besides cotton materials, gems and diamonds, is iron ore, which feeds China's giant steel industry. The answer to correcting this lopsidedness is diversification, and India must seek to push for the export of other commodities as well, particularly those that are in high demand in China. If there are obstructions or artificial barriers to such trade, they can be resolved through the World Trade Organization (WTO) mechanism.

One of the more recent cases of a conflict between India and China had been the standoff at Doklam in 2017. The two sides had been positioned in an eyeball-to-eyeball confrontation, which had escalated tensions. The lesson from that episode is that we must not allow such a situation to be created, and the responsibility for that lies on both sides. Border solutions cannot be found instantly, and the special representatives of both countries must keep working relentlessly to find a way out.

Delivering a lecture in 2016 at the Peking University in China, I had listed eight pillars to resolve bilateral disputes, including the border conflict, using 'civilizational wisdom' and 'political acumen'. These included enhanced political communication, people-to-people contacts through festivals and sporting events, and a common approach to global and developmental issues that facilitate strong cooperation at multilateral forums such as the G20, BRICS, East Asia Summit, Shanghai Cooperation Organization and the Asian Infrastructure Investment Bank (AIIB).

FRIENDSHIP WITH NEPAL

Nepal is among India's closest neighbours. It has a unique relationship with India and there are no border restrictions for people travelling from one country to the other. There is a historic people-to-people relationship that has developed over many centuries, and people of both these nations are connected culturally, religiously and ethnically. Gautam Buddha, a prince of the Shakya clan, was born in Lumbini, Nepal, and passed away in Kushinagar. Six to eight million Nepalese live and work in India. Besides, a number of Nepalese-origin people—the valiant Gorkhas—are recruited in the Indian Army and they comprise the Gorkha Regiment.

Major political developments have taken place in Nepal since the 50s, when King Tribhuvan of the Shah dynasty, which had ruled Nepal for close to 300 years, took shelter at the Indian embassy with the help of the then Indian envoy, C.P.N. Singh, while campaigning to dislodge the Rana dynasty from power. When he flew to New Delhi on an Indian plane that had been especially sent to bring him and his family members in the midst of the tussle that had erupted in Nepal between the Shah and the Rana group—with the latter even anointing Tribhuvan

Singh's four-year-old grandson, Gyanendra, to the throne—the India–Nepal Treaty of Peace and Friendship was signed in 1950. PM Nehru formally welcomed the monarch to India. Over the years, voices have been raised in certain quarters, especially among the political elite of Nepal, over the 'inequitable' nature of the agreement, but no serious attempts were made, including by the Shah rulers, to revise the treaty.

Parliamentary democracy came to Nepal after the Rana dynasty ceased and King Tribhuvan came to power in 1951. The monarchy, however, continued to remain supreme. India–Nepal ties soured in the 17-year reign of King Mahendra (who succeeded King Tribhuvan in 1955). He also dealt a blow to democracy by dissolving Parliament and dismantling the parliamentary form of government. He nominated the PM and constituted the so-called National Panchayat, whose members were handpicked by his court. The country's Army remained largely loyal to the throne, which was critical for the King to sustain his stranglehold. Though overt protests were effectively put down before they even became known, there was simmering discontent, especially in the political establishment. In a realignment aimed at challenging the throne, the Nepali Congress was formed with the merger of the Nepali National Congress and the Nepal Democratic Party. The dominance of feudal politics was especially resented in the largely rural Nepal, leading to the formation of various communist movements, many of which later adopted violent means to achieve their goals. King Mahendra died in 1972 and was succeeded by his son, King Birendra. By then, the communist campaigns had gathered momentum, both in the political and the social spheres. In 1994, Manmohan Adhikari became the PM, heading the country's first elected communist government. Then came Madhav Kumar Nepal, Pushpa Kamal Dahal 'Prachanda' and K.P.S. Oli.

But the road to genuine democracy was never easy in Nepal. The 2001 palace massacre, in which crown prince Dipendra, allegedly under the influence of drugs and alcohol, killed the entire royal family—including King Birendra and Queen Aishwarya—inside the dining hall, played a key role in greatly reducing the pace of democratic changes in the country. King Gyanendra, who took charge, further undermined the mainstream political parties and proceeded to concentrate all powers in himself. Civil unrest and Maoist attacks had broken out, but they were being ruthlessly handled by the Army, which remained loyal to the throne. In October 2002, the King dispensed with even the facade of democracy by dismissing the government and ruling through court-appointed PMs.

New Delhi was understandably worried by developments in its neighbourhood, and that too in a country with which it shared open borders. It was concerned over the growing influence of Maoists, the high-handedness of the royalty and the marginalization of political parties. India did not want the fallout in Nepal to adversely impact its own states, which were dealing with Maoist insurgency. It was an open secret that many Maoist leaders in India had connections with the Maoists of Nepal during their university days in Delhi. India had to tread carefully through the crisis in the neighbourhood. A section of the Nepalese leadership and opinion-makers was hostile to India, spreading the message that the 'big brother' was resorting to 'bullying tactics'. At the same time, there were those who wished to sustain strong ties with India. Incidentally, even those sections that were berating India publicly, sought New Delhi's intervention when it came to the protection of their interests.

Meanwhile, by the beginning of 2005, King Gyanendra had resorted to brinkmanship. He rounded political leaders and put them in prison, and declared a state of emergency. The government of India, which had earlier tried to broker peace between the court and the political parties, now realized the futility of continuing with that process. It strongly criticized the decision of the throne, demanded the release of the political prisoners and suspended military aid to Nepal. But more importantly, it began to work for an understanding between the Maoist groups and the mainstream political parties, so that they could jointly face the throne's challenge. New Delhi's efforts paid off and an agreement, which came to be called the 12-Point Memorandum of Understanding (MoU), was signed by the Maoists and the mainstream political outfits in November 2005. One of the goals was to co-opt the Maoists into the political mainstream. Realizing the grim situation he was in, the king made a show of leniency by releasing a few political prisoners and issuing a statement in favour of multiparty democracy. India quickly welcomed it, not taking into account the fact that several draconian measures to stifle democracy were still in place. But, whatever the case may have been, India was being increasingly seen as an 'interfering' power, and the issue needed to be addressed. Former Indian Foreign Secretary Shyam Saran has, in his book *How India Sees the World*, made a mention of this peculiar situation. As foreign secretary, he had sought my advice, since PM Manmohan Singh was out of the country (he was on a visit to Germany). The issue was: while the PM had called for multiparty democracy in Nepal under a constitutional monarchy, a vast number of people in Nepal resented India's stand since they demanded a complete end of the monarchy. I told him to address a press conference and state that New Delhi would stand by the desire of the people of Nepal. In 1951, it had been the people's will to have multiparty democracy with the monarchy in place, and we had supported it. Now, India supported the Nepalese people's demand for multiparty democracy in a republic.

My advice was not in consonance with the position the PM had taken in his media interaction in Germany. I told the foreign secretary that I would personally explain the matter to the PM on his return to India. Pursuant to my intervention, Saran addressed the media and explained New Delhi's revised stand. He wrote in his book that the announcement was greeted with cheer and celebrations across Nepal. People gathered at the Indian embassy in Kathmandu and demonstrated in support of India. I told the PMO of my decision and when the PM returned, I explained the matter to him. He approved of my initiative wholeheartedly.

Despite the political ups and downs in Nepal over the decades, India has made substantial contribution to the overall development of Nepal—in areas of infrastructure and education, for instance. Roads, bridges, airports, irrigation systems, the East West Highway and the impressive campus of Tribhuvan University in Kathmandu are testimony to India's role. Besides, India has always stood by Nepal in times of natural disasters, helping in every way it can.

Soon after Nepal was hit by a massive earthquake in 2015, PM Modi had moved swiftly to provide assistance, declaring a huge relief and rehabilitation package for the quake-devastated regions. Indian disaster management experts and engineers were also sent to Nepal. India never stopped or cut down on its economic package or developmental assistance to that country. Such assistance has been an intrinsic part of our relationship with Nepal. This, however, was affected during the five-month blockade that rocked Nepal in 2015, but it was not India's doing. The blockade happened in Nepal and was part of the protest movement launched by the Madhesi leadership to press for their demands, including greater political representation and parity with the people in the hills. The agitation was largely in the Terai region through which Indian goods were transported to Kathmandu valley by road. This was not something that the Indian government had resorted to; it was Nepal's internal matter. But even then, certain products such as petroleum were airlifted to Nepal to meet the crisis, though that was not enough. The Nepalese people had to go through tremendous inconvenience caused by the shortfall of a wide range of goods that came from India.

Questions have been raised about how India must manage China's growing influence in Nepal. Given the complex character of the India-Nepal relationship, nothing can be said in affirmative terms. China has been expanding its influence not just in Nepal but countries in Southeast Asia too. We have balanced these relationships in the last 70 years, with occasional stress and strain, and we shall continue to do so. It must be remembered that all countries that have been beneficiaries of massive Chinese aid are apprehensive of Chinese intervention in their internal affairs. It is an old fear and yet they accept Beijing's help to meet their immediate needs. It is true that sometimes they mortgage their future interests in the process.

WORKING WITH SRI LANKA

Sri Lanka and India were administered together till 1947. Soon after India's independence, Ceylon was also made independent, in February 1948. The two new, liberated colonies, despite their huge differences of size and complexity, worked in close cooperation with each other as there were centuries-old cultural linkages between them through Buddhism, the main religion in Sri Lanka. A large number of Indian Tamilians, who had gone from India as plantation workers, settled in central and southern Sri Lanka and constituted a sizeable population of the island. They had an ethnic and cultural bondage with the Tamil population that lived across the bay in India. After independence, during the tenures of Sri Lankan PMs Don Stephen Senanayake and Dudley Senanayake, and Solomon Bandaranaike and his wife Sirimavo Bandaranaike, the India–Ceylon relationship and economic cooperation grew by leaps and bounds.

With a change in the constitutional system in the country after the victory of J.R. Jayawardene, who defeated Sirimavo's party, a presidential form of government was introduced in 1978. Jayawardene, a family friend of Nehru, and himself a participant in the freedom struggle in India, was highly critical of the Emergency imposed by Indira Gandhi. Though the relationship at the political level was under stress, economic cooperation with Sri Lanka in trade, industrialization and the expansion of business continued in the 90s. With the Indo-Sri Lanka Free Trade Agreement signed in 1998, economic cooperation was enhanced manyfold. Bilateral trade, the duty-free exchange of commodity and services, and people-to-people contact increased substantially. In the mid-80s, when SAARC was established, Sri Lanka was an active founding member. India, Bangladesh, Bhutan, Nepal and Pakistan were the other founding members of SAARC. The Maldives joined later and Afghanistan became a full member after the 2008 summit.

The India–Sri Lanka relationship has been greatly influenced by Tamil politics in India, particularly with the emergence of a strong Dravidian party in Tamil Nadu since the mid-60s. A demand was raised by the Tamil population residing on both sides of the Palk Strait that the northern part of Sri Lanka and the southern part of India, having a common cultural and ethnic identity, be brought under the so-called Tamil Eelam. During Rajiv Gandhi's prime ministership, this demand got heightened as the military assistance provided to Sri Lanka by India was used extensively against the Tamil insurgents, particularly the Liberation Tigers of Tamil Eelam (LTTE). Matters deteriorated to such an extent that Rajiv became the victim of a terror attack by the LTTE, under the leadership of V. Prabhakaran. These outfits used to have the tacit support of local governments in Tamil Nadu. (Since 1967, no Congress government has been elected to power in the state with a full majority of its own.) The DMK was the dominant party since then, but the All India Anna Dravida Munnetra Kazhagam (AIADMK), a faction of DMK, headed by the charismatic actor-politician M.G. Ramachandran, emerged as a strong rival of the DMK. Both these Dravidian parties continued to enjoy majority support of the people of Tamil Nadu along with various smaller parties. Therefore, the coastal areas of the state became a safe haven for Tamil terrorists. The government of India used to support them tacitly by overlooking the involvement of Tamil politicians in Sri Lanka's internal matter. This was always an irritant to the Sri Lankan authorities. After Rajiv Gandhi was attacked by a Sri Lankan army man while inspecting a guard of honour during his visit to the island in 1987, the direction to the Indian Army was to help the Sri Lankan government restore law and order in the part of the island that was largely Tamil dominated.

Sri Lankan PM Ranasinghe Premadasa (who also served as president thereafter) was assassinated by an LTTE suicide bomber in May 1993. A number of frontline political leaders, including Vijaya Kumaratunga, husband of former PM Chandrika Kumaratunga, always acted as an irritant to a smooth political relationship. However, this changed substantially when in 1995, I took over as minister for external affairs. During a visit of President Kumaratunga, in the bilateral talks with PM Narasimha Rao, I raised the issue of the extradition of Prabhakaran. We received the cryptic response by the Sri Lankan side that, perhaps, Prabhakaran would not be captured alive, but would be killed before he surrenders. I did, however, bring about a change in our policy, stating that India would like to support the strong anti-terror measures initiated by the Sri Lankan government.

After 1995, the government changed in India. A judicial commission established to look into the conspiracy aspects of Rajiv Gandhi's assassination obliquely hinted at the complicity of the DMK and the Tamil Nadu government in providing logistical support to the Tamil terrorists. The Congress party demanded the expulsion of the DMK from the coalition government at the Centre. The government of I.K. Gujral was dependent on the DMK for survival, and PM Gujral refused to succumb to the Congress's pressure. The government ultimately collapsed, and in the next election, the Congress failed to get a majority, because in Tamil Nadu the party failed to get a single seat. This was the fallout of the Congress's strong anti-Eelam policy. Meanwhile, in Sri Lanka, another important political figure, Foreign Minister Lakshman Kadirgamar, was killed in 2005. I personally attended his funeral, and firmed up my determination to support the Sri Lankan regime's anti-terror operations.

Subsequently, when Mahinda Rajapaksa was elected president, he came to India in June 2010 and had discussions with me and PM Manmohan Singh. I offered India's full support in conducting anti-terror operations. In one of my meetings thereafter, I reached Colombo at 10.30 pm, accompanied by the then national security advisor, Shivshankar Menon, and other senior officials. I drove to the president's house straight from the airport, had discussions with him and senior military personnel on the process of carrying on anti-terror operations, and to simultaneously implement the 13th Amendment of the Sri Lankan Constitution, initiated by Rajiv Gandhi, to arrive at a political settlement between the Sri Lankan Tamils and the Sinhalese. The midnight meeting ended early in the morning. On my return to India, I stopped at Chennai and briefed the then CM, M. Karunanidhi, about the outcome of that meeting.

In my approach to the problem, I repeated to President Rajapaksa and to the Tamil leaders that India would provide substantial support to rehabilitate the internally displaced Tamil population, but the Sri Lankan forces must fight the terrorists on their own; they should not expect Indian soldiers to fight against the terrorists on Sri Lankan soil.

It is true that Rajapaksa allowed Chinese assistance to enter in a massive way in Sri Lanka. Whenever it was objected to by India, he responded by saying that India could then give the massive funds that China gave and implement the projects that the Chinese were willing to do. Naturally, India was on the back foot as it could not compete with China in terms of money. But we repeatedly pointed out to Sri Lanka that India was a trustworthy friend and an immediate neighbour, and the security of the island nation and India was undivided and common because a large number of important nuclear installations and other projects, including the construction of ships and submarines, were located in the southernmost part of India, adjacent to Sri Lanka. It could not turn a blind eye to this aspect. There is no doubt that the massive Chinese presence in the name of infrastructure development in Sri Lanka can cause a serious problem to India's security concerns. That said, I believe that the developmental needs of Sri Lanka must be met more substantially by India, so that Colombo (or any other country placed in a similar situation) cannot use the lack of adequate developmental help from India as an excuse to depend on another country that can pose problems for us.

No Indian PM can overlook the security concerns of this country and, therefore, there is a commonality in pursuing relations, irrespective of the government at the Centre. PM Modi has desired to improve the strained relations of the past.

India also wants to see that the Indian Ocean Region does not become a playground for big powers. This is the reason why India vigorously opposed the naval base of the US at Diego Garcia, in the Indian Ocean and this is the reason why it opposes the excessive designs of China in our backwaters—the Arabian Sea, the Indian Ocean and the Bay of Bengal. The situation offers a true test of diplomacy.

Diplomacy is expected to play a balancing role between conflicting interests and ideas, and through these balancing acts one has to ensure that the national objectives are met.

THE MALDIVES CHALLENGE

We have had a very strong maritime and security relationship with the Maldives, a small island country in the Indian Ocean. In the last few years, tensions grew between the two because of internal political developments in the island country. Apprehensions about Chinese involvement in the Indian Ocean states in India's neighbourhood cannot be understated. Former president, Mohamed Nasheed, tried to counter-balance India's influence in the Maldives by resorting to help and support from China. But with the election of President Ibrahim Mohamed Solih in 2018, the relationship is back on track. PM Modi not only congratulated him on his success but attended his swearing-in as special chief guest. After the Indian PM's first visit, a massive developmental assistance was announced.

BOND WITH AFGHANISTAN

Afghanistan was admitted as the eighth member of SAARC in 2007. Before the partition of India, Afghanistan was the country's frontier to West Asia and Central Asia, and the historic route connecting Peshawar to Kabul is a living monument of the exposure of India to West and Central Asia through this route. Even during the British colonial rule, the relationship between India and Afghanistan constituted a major part of Britain's foreign policy. However, after Partition, Pakistan blocked the road route to India, and Indian trade was severely hampered due to lack of connectivity. The US intervened in Afghanistan to counter the Taliban, and Pakistan was used to fight against the pro-Soviet, Mohammad Najibullah government. Afghanistan was wracked by internal tribal wars for a long period. After international intervention and restoration of the democratic process, India has participated in the development of Afghanistan in a big way through various infrastructure projects. Some of these include the building of Afghanistan's Parliament; the restoration of the Stor Palace in Kabul; the rebuilding of the Habibia High School in Kabul with grants-in-aid; the reconstruction of the Salma dam, now renamed the Afghan–India Friendship Dam; the establishment of a power transmission line; financing the setting up of a national agricultural and technology university; expanding the national television network; and constructing a cricket stadium in Kandahar.

India did not participate in any armed intervention by sending troops to Afghanistan, but it has trained Afghan police and military personnel here. India's investment in Chabahar port in Iran is also part of its efforts to enhance connectivity to Afghanistan. The Zerang-Delaram highway was inaugurated by me, and our relations deepened during my term as president. I believe India–Afghanistan ties are largely trouble-free.

The membership of SAARC has given Afghanistan an opportunity to interact with other SAARC countries and participate in the development process of South Asia by providing links to West and Central Asia.

While on SAARC, I would like to add that the strained relationship between India and Pakistan has come in the way of this regional organization to realize its full potential. More often than not, SAARC summits have been a victim of Indo-Pak disputes. But, despite that, in the recent years, there has been a more proactive role of India in Nepal, Bhutan, Bangladesh and Sri Lanka. Moreover, within SAARC, the regional cooperation among Bangladesh, Bhutan and Nepal has been strengthened. Greater connectivity is one of the agendas being pursued.

AFRICA OUTREACH

Over the years, India has done well to reach out to African countries to strengthen cooperation in areas of trade and economic development. The India–Africa Forum Summit (IAFS) is the official platform for Indo-African trade relations. The first such summit was held in New Delhi in 2008 and was attended by nearly 40 African leaders. Africa has 54 nations and the IAFS is an effective instrument to establish contact and strengthen relationships not only with the member countries but with the whole continent. As president, I undertook visits to some

African countries, including Ghana, Ivory Coast and Namibia. My successor, President Ram Nath Kovind, too has visited a number of African countries. These visits convey a strong message of India's desire and commitment to strengthen its bonds with the African nations.

India can and should use its leverage as a major nation in the region and a leading force of SAARC to achieve its ends. The use of such leverage cannot be prescribed in a rigid formula, but a dynamic foreign policy always takes note of various factors at play and evolves accordingly. The size and economic might of India does create awe and respect, but also some amount of apprehension. At times, India-bashing becomes expedient for some political parties in neighbouring countries to cater to their domestic constituencies. This is something we must not mind too much, nor should we grudge those parties the use of such tactics. We must, however, remain alert and not hesitate to use our leverage in positive ways. The country's leadership should have more bilateral visits involving our neighbours than other nations.

CHAPTER 8

PRESIDENTIAL VISITS ABROAD: REITERATING FRIENDSHIP AND COOPERATION

As President of India, my official visits to foreign countries served many purposes. They demonstrated the close bonds of friendship India had with those nations, signalled India's desire for greater mutual cooperation in varied areas and enhanced the levels of trust and communication. That said, I wanted to limit these visits to a minimum. Before I went on a foreign visit, I used to discuss the issue with the PM. He would send me a letter in which the core points of our bilateral relations were mentioned. It was a practice initiated by PM Modi.

Further, I wished to concentrate on those countries with which India had excellent relationships. On that list, Bangladesh comes first, as a very close and friendly nation. My relationship with Bangladesh developed during the Liberation War of 1971. Even before that, as a student of history, I took keen interest in the political developments within the Muslim League and outside. I also followed the developments in East Pakistan and other parts of Pakistan, including West Punjab, Sindh, North-West Frontier Province and Balochistan. This interest enabled me to play a small role in developing closer links between the two nations. As a minister, I had visited Bangladesh a couple of times. Given my special fondness for the country and understanding of its affairs, I was always involved in India–Bangladesh matters, whether in government or outside during the prime ministership of Deve Gowda, I.K. Gujral and Atal Bihari Vajpayee. Thus, even the non-Congress governments consulted me with regard to Bangladesh affairs.

My family and I have had a close, personal relationship with PM Sheikh Hasina since the time she was in exile in the late 70s in New Delhi. With her return to power for a second time, Sheikh Hasina extended full cooperation to India and prevented extremists from the banned United Liberation Front of Asom (ULFA) to carry out its subversive activities while taking shelter in Bangladesh. This cooperation went to the extent of Bangladeshi authorities arresting the outfit's extremist leader, Golap Baruah alias Anup Chetia, and handing him over to Indian security forces. The Indian government had been trying hard for years to get him extradited. Earlier, Chetia had been arrested by Bangladeshi authorities on a variety of charges, and it was through Sheikh Hasina's personal intervention that his extradition became possible. His arrival in India could further isolate the hardline ULFA leader Paresh Baruah, who, Indian authorities felt, had been leaning towards China and persisting with his anti-India activities.

There is, however, one major issue between the two

countries that remains unresolved: sharing the waters of Teesta. A short recent history on the subject would be in order to grasp the complication. The Teesta, which originates in the Himalayas, is the lifeline of large parts of north Bengal. Bangladesh has sought an 'equitable' distribution of the water to feed its needs and demands, on the lines of the Ganges Water Sharing Treaty of 1996. The Teesta issue hit a roadblock after an attempt was made to resolve it in 1983, with a preliminary arrangement that could not be implemented. Once Sheikh Hasina's Awami League returned to power in 2010, talks resumed between India and Bangladesh. PM Manmohan Singh visited Bangladesh in 2011 and a joint statement was issued, calling on officials of both sides to conclude an interim agreement for the distribution of water on a 'fair and equitable' basis. PM Modi visited Bangladesh in 2015 and there was a revival of hope that the matter would be soon resolved. One of the reasons why the issue remains inconclusive is the string of concerns that West Bengal CM Mamata Banerjee has raised, as the distribution of water would impact her state.

Despite these numerous attempts, I would not say that this is a festering issue, since the term 'festering' has a rather negative connotation. It happens that sometimes water-sharing becomes a problem even among states within the same country, like in India, and special provisions have been made in the Constitution to resolve it. It would be possible to resolve the Teesta water-sharing dispute between India and Bangladesh, now that the general elections are over. However, no Teesta delegation-level discussions have taken place as yet. I have consistently maintained that the issue needs to be resolved through discussion, and this is not such a difficult task given the excellent relations that India and Bangladesh have with each other.

However, another long-standing issue, the Land Boundary Agreement, was resolved by the Modi government in 2015, when the two nations sealed the historic deal to swap territories. This allowed thousands of people living in border regions to choose their nationality after living in uncertainty for decades. The agreement on the ownership of more than 150 enclaves, which had been in limbo due to arrangements made by local rulers centuries ago, concluded one of the most vexing bilateral issues. This was an issue where both countries had very different perceptions on various interrelated issues, such as illegal immigrants and support and indulgence to Indian insurgent groups who took shelter in Bangladesh, and had soured the friendly relations between India and Bangladesh. But the return of Sheikh Hasina to power gave a positive push to the Indo-Bangladesh relation, and talks of enclaves and other related issues were finalized. There had been a possibility of signing these agreements during the visit of Dr Manmohan Singh to Bangladesh, along with some of the CMs of the border states, but somehow it did not happen.

The close bonds I shared with PM Hasina and her family, including her sister, Sheikh Rehana—both of whom had escaped the assassination that had wiped off their family—meant that my elevation as president was greeted with great enthusiasm in Bangladesh. PM Hasina promptly invited me to visit her country at the earliest opportunity. In fact, even during the run-up to the presidential election, I had received several requests to make the trip. After my election, she congratulated me and extended the invite, which I eagerly accepted. Therefore, it was natural for me to visit Bangladesh in 2013 as president of the republic.

No Indian president had visited Bangladesh since 1974. So my visit was historic in more ways than one. Once my aircraft entered the Bangladesh airspace, a couple of planes of that nation's air force escorted it to the airport, where I was received warmly by the PM and her ministers. I was also presented a guard of honour and a 21-gun salute. Later, I had detailed discussions with President Abdul Hamid, PM Hasina and Finance Minister Abul Maal Abdul Muhith. On my part, however, I did my best to create a conducive environment to help resolve the Teesta issue. I had taken a delegation of four Indian MPs, belonging to various political parties, to Bangladesh in order to facilitate a dialogue and a better understanding of the subject, and organized a separate meeting of this group with PM Hasina.

During the visit, an agitation was on in that country, started by large, irate crowds, mostly youth, who were demanding strong action against the members of the Jamaat-i-Islami for their involvement in war crimes during the Liberation War of 1971. These agitators had been born after the liberation struggle. While large parts of the liberation movement have been recorded in publications by the Bangladesh government, many areas have remained unchronicled. I naturally did not visit the sites of the demonstrations, but I followed the events on television. I heard some of the speeches by the agitating leaders and understood the emotions that fuelled their desire. The opposition Bangladesh Nationalist Party leader, Begum Khaleda Zia, too, was scheduled to call on me at my hotel in Dhaka, but she cancelled it at the last moment because she felt the situation on the streets of Dhaka, as a consequence of the ongoing agitation, was not conducive to the safety of her movement.

The President of Bangladesh hosted a dinner for me and my wife, and at a grand ceremony at the Darbar Hall in the Presidential Palace, I was conferred the Bangladesh Muktijuddho Sanmanona (Liberation War award), the country's second highest award. It was, indeed, a great privilege for me to receive the recognition. I was also invited to the University of Dhaka to address a special convocation in which Doctor of Laws, Honoris Causa, was conferred on me. My address to the convocation was widely appreciated, because I delivered it in Bengali and not English.

All my visits to Bangladesh (including the one after my presidency) during Sheikh Hasina's tenure were like a family reunion of sorts for me. I had gone to my father-in-law's house located in a village called Bhadrabila in Narail district. Though my wife had left the place at a very early stage of her life— she must have been five or six years old—she was emotional on visiting the place. The government of Bangladesh had been gracious enough to provide us a helicopter that took us from Dhaka to the village. I was greeted by the villagers, local officials and some of my wife's relatives who were still there. Local television channels covered the visit extensively. Sadly, after this visit, my wife passed away in 2015. PM Hasina came down to attend her funeral.

Following my visit, a number of projects were initiated in the region, such as the Vivekananda Bhaban (students' hostel) at Ramakrishna Mission, Dhaka, which was inaugurated through video-link by PMs Narendra Modi and Sheikh Hasina in 2019.

I also had the opportunity to visit Kuthibari. There is an

Indian connect here. Rabindranath Tagore belonged to a family of big landlords. The Tagore family estate was situated in Shilaidaha village in Bangladesh. He had a boat on which he spent a good deal of his time travelling along the river. His fascination with boats was also evident when he spent a lot of time in the vessel on his trip to Tripura on the invitation of the then maharaja of the region. I was accompanied by Bangladesh's Information Minister Hasanul Haq Inu during my visits to Narail and Shilaidaha.

When PM Hasina visited India in 2017, I had extended an invitation to her to stay at Rashtrapati Bhavan—in the renovated guest wing—and she readily accepted the request. I hosted an official reception for her, and various dignitaries, including West Bengal CM Mamata Banerjee, attended the event. Although she interacted warmly with PM Hasina, her stand on the Teesta water-sharing dispute had not softened.

My visit in 2018 was at the personal invitation of the president of that country and also to participate in the Bangla Sahitya Sammelan held on the premises of the Bangla Academy in Dhaka and jointly organized by other agencies. Hosted by the president, I visited the Bangabandhu Memorial Museum and paid homage to the Father of the Nation, Bangabandhu Sheikh Mujibur Rahman. I was accompanied by the PM's sister, Sheikh Rehana. I also visited Chittagong during this trip, and the University of Chittagong hosted me and conferred a Doctor of Literature degree on me. Among the most memorable of my trips was the one to the birthplace of the great revolutionary, Surya Sen. A former school teacher from Naopoara in Chittagong, Sen, fondly known as 'Master Da', had done the unthinkable feat of liberating Chittagong from British rule for a brief while in April 1930, leading the famous Chittagong Armoury Raid. He was later hanged by the British in 1934. In his memory, the government established a child welfare centre at the site of his residence.

On that occasion, though I was a former president, the security arrangement provided to me and all other facilities extended to me were equal to those given to the head of a state. PM Hasina invited me and my daughter for lunch at her residence. President Abdul Hamid hosted a banquet in my honour. Almost all important ministers and leaders of various political parties called on me and I had fruitful discussions with all of them.

As I look back with fondness at my ties with Bangladesh, I believe that all unresolved issues between the two countries, including that of sharing the Teesta and the Rohingya crisis, can be amicably resolved because we share such a wonderful and deep relationship and that too at the highest levels of political leadership.

TAXATION AND MAURITIUS

My second foreign visit as president was to Mauritius in 2013. After my election as president in 2012, both the then president, Sir Anerood Jugnauth, and PM Navin Ramgoolam congratulated me over the telephone and requested me to visit their country at the earliest opportunity. The issue of the Double Taxation Avoidance Treaty (DTAA) was a major bilateral irritant with Mauritius. It is a bilateral economic agreement between two nations, with an aim to avoid or eliminate double taxation of the same income in two countries. We had differences on the interpretation of certain clauses of the DTAA. The first one, which was signed in 1982, was substantially liberalized during Yashwant Sinha's tenure as finance minister in 1998–99. The Revenue Department of India used to complain that many companies treated Mauritius as a tax haven (internally, Mauritius provided all facilities of a tax haven, and under that agreement many companies doing business and earning huge profits did not pay a single paisa as tax). On enquiry, it was found that they did not pay tax to either Mauritius or India. No doubt this helped small island countries such as Mauritius as a financial hub in the African region. But then, substantial loss of revenue was caused to the Indian exchequer.

I had dealt with this issue both as finance minister and as foreign minister and discussed the matter with Mauritian authorities several times. A series of official-level discussions also took place, but they did not produce much result. We did not want to take any harsh measures (as the agreement could be cancelled by each side after giving requisite notice, as per the agreement of 1982). However, after a great deal of persuasion, a workable solution was eventually arrived at.

During the visit in March 2013, three bilateral agreements—relating to cooperation in the fields of health and medicine, persons with disabilities and senior citizens, and tourism—were signed at Port Louis in the presence of me and PM Ramgoolam. I did not raise the issue of DTAA nor did I talk about it at the delegation level, because we discussed in-depth on developing and strengthening the Indian Ocean Region, with a view to ensure that it does not become a playground for big powers, including China. The US has its base at Diego Garcia, and is involved in some big projects for the development of ports in Sri Lanka. China was also keeping an eye on having its presence in the Indian Ocean, which we believed could lead to a situation similar to the one in the South China Sea at present.

GOODWILL GESTURES

My visits to Belgium and Turkey in October 2013 were essentially bilateral goodwill gestures. There was no specific subject or outstanding issue with either of these countries. Belgium is especially important to India; its capital Brussels houses the headquarters of the European Union (EU) and India has a deep relationship with the EU as a whole. As a bloc, it is the largest trading partner of India, and has had a series of interactions with India during my presidency. However, there was one irritant in our relationship. Sometimes, the representatives of the EU, as such, appeared to be intrusive with regard to India's internal matters relating to J&K. They would frequently ask questions on alleged human rights violations by Indian forces in the state, but they were not very vocal on violations by various terror groups patronized by Pakistan, which indulged in cross-border terrorism. Terrorism itself is the biggest human rights violation, but perhaps they concentrated on violation by government security forces.

I had interactions with King of Belgium, and was hosted by him at a banquet in the Old Fort, where the royal family used to live earlier. The entire ceremonial paraphernalia performed on this occasion. The King and I inspected a guard of honour offered by the Cavalry dressed in the old royal costumes. With the leader from the EU, I had discussions on various bilateral issues and, of course, explained the stated government position on J&K.

In Turkey, I had the wonderful experience of visiting the ancient town of Constantinople, and received an honorary doctorate from the Istanbul University. It is difficult to conceptualize how Turkey is truly both European and Asian. The country is spread between both sides of the Black Sea, which is an extremely narrow strip connecting Europe with Asia.

WOOING MARITIME NATIONS

Apart from its ceremonial aspect, my visit to Vietnam was also emotional in the sense that as a young man coming from West Bengal, the word 'Vietnam' did not connote a mere geographical expression but a symbol of struggle, sacrifice, valour and indomitable spirit against aggression. During my visit, I had detailed discussions with the leaders of Vietnam on bilateral issues. Trade and investments were also discussed at the delegation-level meeting.

In my discussion with both the president and the PM, the problem of the South China Sea and Beijing's role came in for detailed analysis. I shared Vietnam's concerns and assured India's support to Vietnam to maintain the South China Sea as an important international trade route where the flow of trade, commerce and tourists would be uninterrupted. The attempt to convert the international maritime trade route into a domestic lake was disapproved by both the countries. The South China Sea problem continues and also reflects the aggressive role of the Chinese not just in that region, but also in the Indian Ocean as a whole. It is true that China desires to expand its zone of influence further east on to the South China Sea and onwards to the Pacific. If we want to check its aggressive maritime policy, including in the Indian Ocean, the only way to do so is by building closer relationships with maritime countries. India must develop and expand military ties with South Asian and Southeast Asian countries to maintain the safety and security of international maritime trade routes.

I had the opportunity to inaugurate the India Study Centre in Ho Chi Minh National Academy for Politics and Public Administration in September 2014 at Hanoi. In my speech, I stressed upon the strong civilizational bonds that existed between India and Vietnam:

> Strong civilizational bonds [have existed] between India and Vietnam since the second century. These have, today, evolved into a vibrant and multidimensional strategic partnership. Our current dialogue is based on the close understanding and friendship of the founding fathers of our two great nations. India and Vietnam have had similar experiences in shaping our national identities—our struggle for freedom from colonial rule, our thirst for development and the realization of the aspirations of our people.

President Ho Chi Minh had likened the India–Vietnam relationship to a 'cloudless sky'. Today, our bilateral dialogue is frank and our cooperation in areas of common interest has grown from strength to strength. We are engaged in joint initiatives and programmes across a wide range of areas of common interest. In 2012, we also celebrated the 40th anniversary of the establishment of our diplomatic relations.

NORDIC DIPLOMACY

Norway has always been known as a peace-loving country; it is traditionally against any expansion of nuclear weapons and is an ardent supporter of nuclear non-proliferation. During my visit to the country in 2014, I also wanted to impress upon the leadership that while India had signed the 123 Agreement (civil nuclear cooperation agreement) with the US, it was essentially done for producing nuclear energy to meet the energy deficiency of the country. India's commitment to nuclear disarmament and non-proliferation is total. As the external affairs minister, when I negotiated the treaty with the US and spoke to various countries for providing a one-time exception to India from the NSG, I underlined India's commitment to total nuclear disarmament to prevent and reduce stockpiling, as the country's traditional policy.

In Finland, I saw a remarkable change the country has undergone since the late 90s. In 1995, my visit to Finland was aimed at enhancing the supply of paper pulp for the production of newsprint. During my visit as president, I discovered that Finland had altogether given up the paper trade and they were concentrating on preserving forests and wood products. Clearly, they believed that the protection of environment was more important than any sectoral development at the cost of the environment.

In my address at Helsinki to an audience of businesspersons in October 2014, I said that the gathering would not only help develop business contacts between India and Finland but also assist in deepening mutual understanding and interaction. On the business front, I pointed out that the Indo-Finnish Joint

Commission was an important forum to take this task forward. I added:

> In addition, there are several sector-specific initiatives, like a Memorandum of Cooperation in the Road Transportation sector, S&T Cooperation Agreement and an MoU between the Department of Science and Technology of India and TEKES, the Finnish funding agency for technology and innovation. An Indo-Finnish Working Group on Innovation was created in 2011. Both countries have also signed an agreement for cooperation in the field of Information Security. A Joint Working Group on Environment has been holding regular meetings and another Joint Working Group on Clean Technology and Waste Management has been set up.

Developing deeper relations with the Nordic countries was not limited to geography and culture. Most of these countries belong to the European security regime or the North Atlantic Treaty Organization, which is essentially against India's non-aligned policy. As part of this policy, India does not believe that there should be a bloc of nations pitted against another bloc. We firmly believe that the UN and its Security Council, under Chapter 7, have to ensure the security of the world as a whole, and there should be parity with the UN mandate through implementing the collective decisions of the nations in the UN. However, we do work in close cooperation with Nordic countries towards economic growth, innovation and climate change. For example, Finland was an important supplier of newsprint to India and now, with respect to climate change, India is closely working with various other Nordic countries. Also, in the field of communication, a number of companies—Nokia, for instance—located in Finland, are working in India.

During my official visit to Sweden in 2015, a number of agreements on sustainable developments and innovation were signed between the countries. Sweden is essentially an innovation-led economy, and for a very long period of time, Swedish companies have been making investments in India.

The visit also provided me an opportunity to speak on the relevance of Rabindranath Tagore and Mahatma Gandhi in the quest for global peace. Addressing a gathering at the Uppsala University in Stockholm in June, I reminded the audience of the increased relevance of these two great sons of the soil in the present times of strife. I brought to their attention the sterling role played by one of their own in the campaign for peace. I said:

> ...this hallowed centre of studies nurtured Dag Hammarskjöld, a great Swede and the second Secretary-General of the United Nations...the youngest to have held the post. His contributions to the cause of peace brought him respect and popularity across the world. I wonder how many of you know that this noble diplomat was also blessed with immense spiritual wisdom. One of his legacies at the United Nations is the creation of the Room of Quiet, which exists to this day. Dag Hammarskjöld was aware that the first step towards finding peace outside is to find it within. He knew that meditation and quiet are important conditions for this quest.

I expressed gratitude on behalf of India to the University of

Uppsala for having installed a bust of Tagore in its Department of Foreign Languages. This bust commemorates the centenary of the awarding of the Nobel Prize to Tagore and stands as a reminder of his special link to Uppsala. I expressed delight 'that 27 of Tagore's works have been translated into Swedish and are widely appreciated'.

I told the gathering:

> Rabindranath Tagore was a renaissance man and such men are found rarely in history. In their personality, they capture not just the times they live in but also many complex questions that transcend geography and are pertinent for all countries and communities across the world. Tagore's views on 'nationalism' reveal his distaste for parochialism, racial divide and social stratification. He firmly believed that world peace could never be achieved until big and powerful nations curbed their desire for territorial expansion and control over smaller nations. In his view, war was a consequence of aggressive Western materialism that developed in the early part of the 20th century, with science divorced from spirituality.

Tagore's advocacy for global peace appealed to the intellectual sections of society in India and abroad. Mahatma Gandhi, too, was a votary of peace, and he launched a unique campaign to achieve freedom from colonial rule centred on the deployment of truth and non-violence. He derived moral stature by leading from the front. Indira Gandhi had once observed: 'He was one of those who spoke as he thought and acted as he spoke, one of those few on whom no shadow fell between word and deed.

His words were deeds, and they built a movement and a nation, and changed the lives of countless individuals.'

I concluded my address in Sweden by observing that the ideas of 'truth, openness, dialogue and non-violence' espoused by these two great leaders and thinkers were even more relevant today, in a world confronted with growing intolerance and terrorism.

A DEPENDABLE NEIGHBOUR

My standalone visit to Bhutan in 2014 reflected the deep relationship between India and our Himalayan neighbour. Since the early 90s, as deputy chairman of the Planning Commission, I was personally involved in the developmental activities of Bhutan. Hydropower projects implemented by India in that country have proved to be highly beneficial to both the countries, as India meets its energy requirements from the power supply by Bhutan, and Bhutan earns substantial revenue and employment-generation through these projects. The FYPs of Bhutan are substantially financed by India, of which a large component is aid, and the other component is soft loans.

India and Bhutan have shared many common perceptions in the international arena, and Bhutan is India's steady partner in most of the international issues affecting our two nations. The solution to the Doklam stand-off came through mutual discussions between India and China, with Bhutan being firmly on the Indian side. India and Bhutan have shared perceptions—militarily, politically and economically. This bonhomie was reinforced during the golden jubilee celebrations in 2018, marking the establishment of diplomatic relations and were conducted with enthusiasm through various activities in both countries.

HISTORIC VISITS

One country with which India has had perhaps the longest-standing friendly relation is Russia. The friendship goes back to the Soviet era. Throughout the 60s, 70s and early 80s, India received massive developmental support from Russia in building its heavy industries, steel plants and machine tools. Bokaro, Bhilai and Ranchi are the monuments of this cooperation. Today, Russia is India's dependable partner in all sectors, including defence and energy. The Indo-Russian relationship has stood the test of time.

My visit to Russia as president in 2015 was to renew and re-emphasize this aspect of our relationship, and synchronized with the 70th anniversary celebrations of that country's victory in World War II. Vladimir Putin extended an invitation to me and I accepted it. The Victory Day parade also witnessed the participation of a 70-member Indian Army contingent from the Grenadiers. As external affairs minister in May 1995, I had, at the invitation of the then president of the Union of Soviet Socialist Republics (USSR), Boris Yeltsin, the privilege of attending the 50th anniversary of the Victory Day parade at Red Square. I witnessed the parade of the veterans of the World War II, which was a marvellous show, since most of them were in their seventies.

During my visit, I was advised by PM Modi to have detailed discussions with Putin on aspects ranging from civil nuclear cooperation and space to the process of delivering defence hardware, including Sukhoi-30 and other sensitive equipment, as well as higher education. We also signed several agreements to extend cooperation in different fields of activities. I felt the warmth of President Putin when I had a one-on-one meeting with him and assured him that our relationship, which had been built over decades, would not be affected by any other relationship (especially the close cooperation on civil nuclear energy with the US, by signing the 123 Agreement).

We also discussed Russia's relationship with China and Pakistan. There has been some concern that the recent warming up of the relationship between Russia and Pakistan has been at India's cost and that Moscow is veering away from New Delhi. My discussions with Putin assumed significance, especially because when I had met him for the first time as India's defence minister, he had assured me that Russia would not have any arms deal with Pakistan. Regardless of this development, I still believe that Russia's relationship with other countries does not stand in the way of the India–Russia friendship. In this regard, one must mention that the balance of power has ceased to be an important instrument of diplomacy following the end of the Cold War. The balance of power was relevant when the world was polarized between two major power blocs—the US and the USSR. Therefore, diplomacy has to be conducted in this new perspective without carrying the old baggage. India has done well through different governments to take this diplomacy forward.

The discussions were followed by a gala dinner hosted by President Putin, and all the heads of the state attended the 70th anniversary celebrations. I had bilateral discussions with quite a few leaders, including President Mahmoud Abbas of Palestine. He extended an open invitation to me to visit Palestine and said, 'Whether you combine it with a visit to Israel or any other country, you are always a welcome guest in Palestine.' In principle, I accepted his invitation, which was later finalized as a visit to three countries—Jordan, Palestine and Israel. I also had a series of discussions with the presidents of most of the Central Asian republics. We discussed the Turkmenistan-Afghanistan-Pakistan-India (TAPI) project, which I consider my dream project. I also met the President of Ukraine.

During this state visit, I delivered a lecture at the prestigious Russian Diplomatic Academy and they conferred an Honorary Doctorate on me. I also inaugurated a festival of Indian culture in Moscow, called 'Namaste Russia'. I visited the Moscow State University and launched the Network of Indian and Russian Universities. I reminded the gathering that India and Russia had a long history of educational cooperation. In the late 50s, the Soviet Union supported the Indian Institute of Technology, Bombay, in its formative years. Tens of thousands of Indian students studied in Russia in the 70s, 80s and 90s. Though the numbers had dropped somewhat in recent years, over 4,000 Indian students studied at Russian universities, I said. As far back as 1930, during his visit to the Soviet Union, Rabindranath Tagore had described Russian universities as 'miracles in the realm of education'. It is this educational system that led to Russia's enviable success as a nation of learning and enabled its technological achievements in areas such as material sciences, aerospace, nuclear science, petrochemicals, mining and heavy engineering.

I emphasized the need for a broader and institutionalized

engagement between educational institutions of India and Russia. The setting up of a Network of Indian and Russian Universities would facilitate the establishment of more institutional linkages, including exchanges of faculty, researchers and students, joint research activities and scientific conferences and symposia.

I used my visit to also interact with researchers in Indology. I said that their efforts had contributed to creating a greater understanding of India's culture and civilization among Russians, and added that the younger generation of researchers should be encouraged to undertake similar studies by giving it contemporary relevance and making the effort professionally rewarding. In this context, I announced that the ICCR would institute an annual Distinguished Indologist award for promoting Indology abroad, and that it would organize a regional conference on Sanskrit and Indology in Russia.

My presidential visit to Russia ended on a very satisfactory note. I was particularly happy that many of the processes that I had initiated as defence, commerce and external affairs minister had fructified, and new areas of cooperation were initiated with Russia.

In a statement that was issued on the conclusion of my visit, I thanked the leadership and the people of that country for their warmth and friendliness. I said, 'During my long decades in public life, I have interacted with the leadership of Russia in many capacities on key issues such as the Rupee-Rouble Agreement and defence and civil nuclear cooperation. I have known President Putin for over 15 years, and have had the pleasure of receiving him twice in Delhi since I assumed office.'

Conveying India's best wishes to President Putin and the

friendly people of Russia, I noted that the visit—the first by me as President of India—had been truly memorable. It had helped deepen our bilateral relations. I expressed confidence that the India–Russia partnership would scale new and even more glorious heights in the days to come.

My visit to Israel and Palestine in 2015 was historic; it was the first-ever visit by an Indian president, which also saw the 'either-Israel-or-Palestine scenario' undergoing a change. India is the first non-Arab country to recognize the Palestine Liberation Organization as the sole and legitimate representative of the Palestinian people and is one of the first countries to recognize the Palestinian State. But we also believe the problems between Israel and Palestine have to be resolved as per the UN resolution and that eastern Jerusalem should be part of Palestine. Violence between Israel and Palestine is almost a daily occurrence, and during my visit, no doubt, it was accentuated. I did not make Israel a standalone visit since that could have sent a wrong message to our friends in the region. It was clubbed with my visits to Palestine and Jordan to convey the message that India wanted the resolution of all outstanding issues between Israel and Palestine through peaceful dialogue as per the UN resolution.

Our relationship with Israel has helped us augment the supply of sophisticated electronic equipments and instruments needed for our defence forces. In the field of space and electronics, our companies are working in close cooperation with Israeli companies. The reciprocal visit in 2016 of the Israeli President Reuven Rivlin to India after my trip, and the subsequent visit of PM Modi the following year and the in-depth discussions he had with his Israeli counterpart Benjamin Netanyahu—with whom he shares a close friendship—have further strengthened the relationship between the two nations.

My trip as president to New Zealand (and Papua New Guinea) in 2016 took place more than 20 years after Rajiv Gandhi visited the country as PM. I had visited that country as the head of the Indian delegation to attend the Commonwealth Heads of Government Meet (CHOGM) in 1995. PM Narasimha Rao could not attend this conference, so I had to represent him in Auckland, which hosted the event. New Zealand is a small but developed country, and in the 50s and 60s, large quantities of milk and milk products were imported by India from there, a part of which was food aid to India. After India became self-sufficient and an exporter of milk products, the trade in this commodity with New Zealand ceased. But in certain other areas, particularly in the use of non-conventional energy, New Zealand still has an important role. In the education sector, a large number of Indian students and teachers are engaged in various universities there, and this small Indian community living there is highly respected by and cooperative with the local government.

My visit to Papua New Guinea was the first-ever by a head of state. It is a highly forest-rich country and, though distance stands in the way of our expanding relationship, I feel it is high time we develop closer ties with this island economy.

DECODING CHINA

India and China are two great Asian countries. Since we re-established our full diplomatic relationship and began cooperation in trade and investment in the early 90s, the Sino–Indian relationship has assumed a critical role in our external relations. Of course, we have the long-standing problem of border settlement, and after a series of discussions through the office of the special representatives tasked with finding solutions, the two nations are working peacefully to achieve that goal.

China has always been sensitive to the issue of the Dalai Lama, the spiritual leader who was given refuge in India during Nehru's tenure as PM. His activities are always looked at with suspicion by Beijing. The issue remains a thorn in our bilateral relationship, though we have repeatedly said that he has been given shelter as a religious leader and not as a political activist. A substantial number of his followers live in India. As a person, he has endeared himself to many others during his long presence in India and through his sobering approach on various conflicting issues affecting the world. In fact, many consider him as a messenger of peace and inclusivity and truly an embodiment of Buddha's message of love, affection and harmony. My meeting with him at Rashtrapati Bhavan was absolutely in my personal capacity, and I made this clear to the Chinese authorities during my visit to China in May 2016.

In 2008, when the Olympic torch passed through India, there were reports that Tibetans settled in India would demonstrate against China's unlawful occupation of Tibet. As the external affairs minister, I assured my counterpart in China that the torch would receive a smooth passage. I spoke to him over the phone a couple of times and when he came to India, I also told him of the security arrangements, which he greatly appreciated. But I remember that, during that conversation I raised the issue of his apprehension of the mischief that could be done by the 'Dalai clique'. I know it is a sensitive issue for China, but it is equally true that India has been known for its hospitality towards guests who have taken shelter in this country. The Dalai Lama entered India at a very young age in the 50s, and through all these years, he has received appreciation for his work; in recognition of that, he was awarded the Nobel Peace Prize in 1989.

My visit to China in 2016, one of the last visits I undertook as president, was important for several reasons. The trip to Guangzhou was highlighted by the business delegation that accompanied me. The delegation had very productive meetings with its counterparts and a large number of MoUs were signed between the companies concerned. A roundtable conference was held in Beijing, where various aspects of the Sino–Indian relationship, including cultural exchange and institutional arrangements to promote people-to-people contacts, were discussed. It was my practice to take a number of vice chancellors of Indian universities with me in my delegation, who used to have discussions with their counterparts in the visiting country. In Beijing, vice chancellors of Indian universities and the presidents of the Chinese universities met at the roundtable at Peking University. The discussions were productive and instrumental in furthering cooperation in the field of education. A number of MoUs were signed between Indian universities and their counterparts in China.

The issue of Maulana Masood Azhar, wanted by India, did not appear to be that important. But the menace of terrorism and its pernicious effects all over the world, cutting across geographical, religious and cultural borders, did form a part of the discussions.

I thanked China for its support in extending a one-time

exception to the NSG clearance to facilitate the signing of the 123 Agreement. While I thanked President Xi Jinping, I also focussed on the need for facilitating India to be a regular member of the NSG. At the formal banquet, President Xi and I were seated side by side. Also present was an interpreter and Yang Jiechi, who was known to me when he was vice minister, Ministry of Foreign Affairs; later on, he became the special representative of President Xi in resolving the border dispute between India and China. In the dinner, which was more than an hour long, President Xi began a discussion on historical issues and asked me to explain to him the functioning of the government of India in its constitutional framework, implementation of policies and the mechanism through which they are put into operation. He raised a host of questions and sought answers. Even though I spoke in English, he did not want the interpreter's assistance to translate my observations, except on occasions when I discussed the McMahon Line. It was an interesting situation: long discussions were happening between President Xi and me without the help of an interpreter, and none of the guests around had an inkling of what was being talked about! Our then Foreign Secretary, S. Jaishankar, commented to Secretary Omita Paul that the two presidents were involved in a discussion for more than an hour without anybody knowing what was being discussed. After the dinner, Jaishankar rushed to me and asked if anything important had been discussed. I told him that the only important thing was that one had to revisit the story of India's Constitution and its functioning since the 50s!

Disputes and differences apart, both India and China are interested in the rejuvenation of the Asian Century. In fact, the two countries would be the biggest beneficiaries as the largest economies of Asia. They understand that the way forward is to deepen bilateral cooperation and not let differences impact progress. Of course, China will be at the forefront of the economic might several folds more than India. But India is also moving fast.

To rejuvenate the Asian Century, we must work hard along with other Asian countries and the institutional framework of cooperation with the Association of Southeast Asian Nations (ASEAN), strengthening the grouping in the process. The participation and involvement in these structures must be deepened. Moreover, bilateral issues between India and Pakistan, China and maritime nations around the South China Sea, and other regional disputes should be resolved peacefully and amicably.

AFRICAN POSSIBILITIES

Though the African continent provides huge opportunities for Indian investment and trade, and bilateral and multilateral economic cooperation possibilities between African nations and India are vast, we have not been able to fully utilize those opportunities. Personally, my own exposure to African countries was very limited. I had visited South Africa and re-established our trade ties, which stood suspended since 1947. In 1994, at the end of Apartheid, I was commerce minister at the Centre. Thereafter I visited some other African countries—Morocco, Libya, Egypt, Uganda and Tanzania—in my capacity as external affairs minister, commerce minister and finance minister. But I had still not gone to a vast part of the continent. So, as president, when the opportunities came, I visited Ghana, Ivory Coast and Namibia in June 2016.

Ghana's Kwame Nkrumah was a leading light along with Nehru, Egyptian leader Gamal Abdel Nasser and Yugoslavia's Josip Broz Tito, of the Non-Aligned Movement (NAM). Ivory Coast was also an important African country and India supported its liberation movement. Namibia was one of the last countries that was liberated in 1990. India solidly supported the liberation movement of Namibia under the leadership of Sam Nujoma. The New Delhi Declaration of the 7th NAM summit held under the chair of Indira Gandhi had contained an emphatic demand for the liberation of Namibia.

I can say with some amount of satisfaction that my visits to the African countries towards the end of my presidency were fruitful and productive. In fact, as president, I supplemented the efforts of the government in building better economic cooperation and improvement of relations with the African nations.

The selection of the countries I needed to travel to as president was left to the Ministry of External Affairs (MEA), and I carried forward the brief the government provided to me. In this regard, it must be remembered that the PM is expected to involve the president in all major international events, as per the constitutional requirements. During my days as president, PM Modi kept me informed of the major events with regard to our international relations.

In all my travels, I made it a point to interact with journalists, whether on my way abroad or my return. I believe that the media needs to be given a factual picture; else there is always scope for needless speculation. I also sought responses from the media, thus ensuring a free flow of information both ways. I, thus, had mediapersons—besides my own officials, representatives from the academia and officials from government departments—accompany me on the foreign visits. The composition of the delegation was dependent on the nature and agenda of the visit.

PM Sheikh Hasina greets my wife, Suvra, during our visit to Bangladesh in 2013.

Receiving a traditional welcome at Bhadrabila village in Bangladesh in 2013.

Bidding adieu to PM Sheikh Hasina on my departure from Hazrat Shahjalal International Airport, Bangladesh, in 2013.

Proposing a toast with Veena Ramgoolam, wife of the PM of Mauritius, Navinchandra Ramgoolam, at a banquet hosted by the him in Port Louis in 2013.

Laying a wreath at the mausoleum of Turkey's first president, Mustafa Kemal Ataturk, at Ankara, Turkey, in 2013.

Celebrating my birthday in 2013 on board Air India's special aircraft in the presence of Sushma Swaraj (left), Satish Misra (behind me; left), Sonia Gandhi (behind me; right) and Sitaram Yechury

Recep Tayyip Erdoğan, PM of Turkey, calls on me at Ankara in 2013.

Posing for a group photograph with King Philippe and Queen Mathilde of Belgium on the stairs of the Royal Palace of Brussels in 2013.

Meeting the King of Bhutan, Jigme Khesar Namgyel Wangchuck, in Thimphu in 2014.

Being escorted by Queen Sonja for a banquet hosted by King Harald V and the Queen at the Royal Palace in Oslo, Norway, in 2014. Also seen is my daughter, Sharmistha.

Proposing a toast with Truong Tan Sang, President of Vietnam, at the Presidential Palace in Hanoi in 2014.

Performing a puja during a visit to the Ben Duoc Memorial Temple in Ho Chi Minh City, Vietnam, in 2014.

With Sauli Niinistö, President of Finland, and Jenni Haukio, the First Lady of Finland, before the ceremonial banquet at the Government Palace in Helsinki in 2014.

Shaking hands with Vladimir Putin, President of the Russian Federation, at the Kremlin, Moscow, in 2015.

With King Carl XVI Gustaf and Queen Silvia of the Kingdom of Sweden at the Royal Palace in Stockholm in 2015.

Greeting King Abdullah II at the Al Husseiniya Palace in Amman, Jordan, in 2015.

After the wreath-laying ceremony at the Victory Monument at the Victory Square in Minsk, Belarus, in 2015.

In conversation with Israeli PM Benjamin Netanyahu (left) and President Reuven Rivlin at a state dinner during my historic visit to Israel in 2015.

Discussing the future of India's relations with the State of Palestine, with President Mahmoud Abbas, at the presidential palace in 2015.

Inspecting a guard of honour with President Xi Jinping during the ceremonial welcome at the Great Hall of the People in Beijing, China, in 2016.

Receiving the traditional dress material of Côte d'Ivoire (Ivory Coast) from Robert Beugré Mambé (to my left), Governor of Abidjan, during a presentation ceremony in Abidjan in 2016.

Witnessing a cultural performance during the ceremonial reception at the State House of the Republic of Namibia in 2016. Also seen is Namibian president, Hage Geingob (to my left).

Delighted at a performance by tribal artists at a banquet hosted by the Governor-General of Papua New Guinea, Sir Michael Ogio, in the capital city of Port Moresby in 2016.

Being welcomed in traditional Maori style by Gregory Baughen, official secretary to the Governor General of New Zealand at Government House, Auckland, in 2016.

Reaffirming the vision for a strong and stable Afghanistan: With President of Afghanistan, Hamid Karzai, at a banquet in his honour at Rashtrapati Bhavan in 2012. Also seen are UPA Chairperson, Sonia Gandhi (centre); Minister of External Affairs, Salman Khurshid (right of Karzai); and Congress General Secretary, Rahul Gandhi (next to me).

With the heads of state/government at the ASEAN India Commemorative Summit at Rashtrapati Bhavan in 2012. Also seen are PM Manmohan Singh (second from my left) and Vice President M. Hamid Ansari (second from my right).

PM Manmohan Singh and I welcome Emomali Rahmon, President of Tajikistan, in 2012.

Welcoming the President of Ukraine, Viktor Yanukovych, to Rashtrapati Bhavan in 2012.

In an animated conversation with King Juan Carlos I of Spain at Rashtrapati Bhavan in 2012.

Greeting the First Lady of Burundi, Denise Bucumi Nkurunziza, as her husband, President Pierre Nkurunziza, looks on, during their state visit to India in 2012.

The Morsy Code: Greeting Mohamed Morsy, Egypt's first democratically elected president, during his state visit to India in 2013.

With the President of Egypt, Abdel Fattah el-Sisi, in 2016.

At the ceremonial banquet in honour of President of Liberia, Ellen Johnson Sirleaf, at the Rashtrapati Bhavan in 2013.

Presenting a gift to Emperor Akihito and Empress Michiko of Japan, during their visit to India in 2013. This was the first time that an emperor and empress of Japan visited our country.

Son of the soil: PM Manmohan Singh (right) and I with the President of Mauritius, Rajkeswur Purryag, in 2013. It was an emotional homecoming for President Purryag who visited his ancestral village in Patna, Bihar.

King of Bhutan, Jigme Khesar Namgyel Wangchuck, greets my wife, Suvra, at the lawns of the Rashtrapati Bhavan in 2013. Also seen is Vice President, M. Hamid Ansari (in the back; left).

King of Bhutan, Jigme Khesar Namgyel Wangchuck, listens intently to my words of advice during his visit to India in 2014. His wife and Queen of Bhutan, Jetsun Pema, looks on.

Neighbourhood first: Welcoming the President of Sri Lanka, Mahinda Rajapaksa, during his visit to India in 2014 to attend the swearing-in of PM Narendra Modi in May that year.

Presenting a book to Peng Liyuan, wife of Chinese President Xi Jinping, in 2014, as he looks on.

Meeting the President of South Korea, Park Geun-hye, as she arrives for a ceremonial reception at Rashtrapati Bhavan during her state visit in 2014.

Strengthening India's ties with the Kingdom of Bahrain during the visit of the King of Bahrain, Hamad bin Isa Al Khalifa, in 2014.

With the President of the Maldives, Abdulla Yameen Abdul Gayoom, as he speaks to the media in the forecourt of the Rashtrapati Bhavan during his visit in 2014.

In conversation with Joachim Gauck, President of Germany, during the ceremonial banquet in Rashtrapati Bhavan in 2014.

A new chapter in Indo-US relations: With President Barack Obama and First Lady Michelle Obama at the Rashtrapati Bhavan in 2015.

A warm welcome awaits Mohammad Ashraf Ghani, President of Afghanistan, on a state visit to India in 2015.

PM Narendra Modi and I with President James Alix Michel of the Seychelles at the forecourt of Rashtrapati Bhavan in 2015.

President of Singapore, Tony Tan Keng Yam, and his wife, Mary Chee Bee Kiang, are enthralled by the majesty of the Rashtrapati Bhavan during their visit to India in 2015.

In the middle of an intense discussion with the President of France, Francois Hollande, the chief guest of our Republic Day celebrations in 2016.

Sharing a light moment with the President of Kyrgyzstan, Almazbek Atambayev, in 2016. First Lady Raisa Atambayeva is seen behind him, smiling.

Hosting the President of Myanmar, Htin Kyaw, and his wife, Daw Su Su Lwin, at the Rashtrapati Bhavan in 2016. Also seen are PM Narendra Modi (right); External Affairs Minister, Sushma Swaraj (behind me; left); and former PM Manmohan Singh (behind me).

Taking the salute at the guard of honour ceremony for the Crown Prince of Abu Dhabi, Sheikh Mohammed bin Zayed Al Nahyan, in 2016.

Reliving the age-old connection of history, culture, tradition and religion with the President of Nepal, Bidya Devi Bhandari, in 2017.

A new high in a historic relationship: With the President of Cyprus, Nicos Anastasiades, at the Rashtrapati Bhavan in 2017.

Presenting a souvenir to the President of Kenya, Uhuru Kenyatta, on his state visit to India in 2017.

CHAPTER 9

INTERACTING WITH LEADERS: OF HEADS OF STATE AND GOVERNMENT

Interactions of the President of India with the heads of state or government of different countries normally take place during their visits to India or on ceremonial occasions, like our Republic Day parade or the national day of some other country. When the president visits as an invited guest to that country, he naturally has an opportunity to interact with the head of that country/ government and usually agreements are signed for cooperation between the two nations in the presence of the visiting dignitary and the head of the state of the receiving country. Therefore, every interaction with the head of state must be reviewed in the perspective mentioned above. In countries such as the US, the president is the head of state and also the executive functionary of the country. In other cases, such as India, the president has a non-executive role. I had the privilege of interacting with a large number of such dignitaries, both in India and abroad, during the course of my presidentship.

The choice of a chief guest for the Republic Day parade is essentially a political decision taken by the government in consultation with the president. The cabinet finalizes the name and the PM then discusses with the president. This practice has been followed since 26 January 1950. PMs and presidents have come and gone, but the practice continues and has become customary.

It is also customary that every chief guest of the Republic Day event is hosted at a banquet by the president before 26 January, i.e., 24/25 January. At that time, the president takes the opportunity of discussing with the guest our bilateral relations—salient features and ways to advance them. Major international issues are also discussed.

During this event, the preparation of the guest list and menu to be served either at the banquet or for the president's 'At Home' are decided by the hospitality section of the Presidential Office, which is under the control of the military secretary to the president. The secretary to the MEA and the PM are also consulted, because on certain occasions (like for Barack Obama's banquet), several guests sought an invitation. So we had to curtail the list. Before the construction of the new hospitality section in the new Presidential House annexe building, the accommodation for the banquet was extremely limited, as the main banquet room could house just 80 persons. However, with the construction of the new annexe, a larger number of guests could be accommodated for the banquet. The new facilities are being largely utilized by the president and the PM.

THE PRESIDENTIAL YEARS

BHUTAN: EXTRAORDINARILY SPECIAL

In 2013, the King of Bhutan, His Majesty Jigme Khesar Namgyel Wangchuck, was the chief guest at our Republic Day event. This visit was a reflection of the prospering relationship between the two countries. He ascended the throne in 2006 when the incumbent King Jigme Singye Wangchuck voluntarily decided to step down and instal his son to the throne. Before that, the young Crown prince (fifth in line) was undergoing military training and studying in New Delhi. Thus, everyone here knew him well, and he too knew and had interacted with Indian politicians.

I have had a personal rapport and intimacy with the royal family of Bhutan since the early 90s. My first visit to the Himalayan kingdom took place when I was deputy chairman of the Planning Commission, at the invitation of King Jigme Singye, to finalize the Government of India's assistance to Bhutan's FYPs. Particularly in that year, large chunks of the development assistance were in the form of grants and a small component was by way of a loan. Since then, I visited Bhutan several times, and each time I had the honour of being hosted by Their Majesties the King and the Queen. During my tenure as defence minister, the then Crown prince Jigme Khesar spent a year in New Delhi while attending the 45th course of the National Defence College in 2005. In 2007, he and I (then serving as the external affairs minister) signed the revised Indo-Bhutan Friendship Treaty. The first such treaty was signed in 1949. Before inking the revised treaty, we had a long discussion with the King for nearly two hours. It was a closed-door meeting between him, PM Manmohan Singh and me. The PM and I represented the Government of India and the King spoke on behalf of Bhutan. He did not take the help of any aides, but his son, as Crown prince, was present during the entire discussion. We were not very eager to revisit the treaty signed in 1949, as we apprehended that it may reopen a Pandora's Box. But the King insisted. Rather bluntly, I told him, 'We are vitally interested in preserving the concept of joint security of India and Bhutan; in fact, the security aspect of both the countries is common and indivisible.' This had been going on since 1949, and the King himself shared the common security concept between India and Bhutan when he led the fight to wipe out terrorists of the north-eastern region who had taken shelter in some parts of Bhutan and were carrying on their anti-India activities. When I emphasized this point, Dr Singh supported me strongly and requested the King to reconsider the whole issue and not insist on a revision of the treaty.

However, his counter-argument was that the concept of common security between India and Bhutan had developed over the years and had become part of convention. But he was now providing a draft treaty that took into consideration a common security concept. Article 2 of the treaty explicitly admitted that the security of both the countries was interlinked and inseparable. All through the almost two hours of discussion, the Crown prince was present, but he did not utter a single word and showed exemplary discipline in not speaking on any issue. Much later, I congratulated him on his model conduct.

On that day, after prolonged discussions, we informed the King that we should ponder independently on our respective viewpoints and meet again. He agreed and the meeting was adjourned. Finally, when we agreed to revise the treaty, he suggested that the revised treaty be signed by the Crown prince on behalf of Bhutan and me as the external affairs minister on India's behalf. When I protested that the Crown prince was higher to me in protocol, the King laughed and said, 'Doesn't matter; our relationship is not only special but it is extraordinarily special.'

Both the kings have had immense trust in me. I had the honour to advise King Jigme Singye when democracy was introduced in Bhutan. Even when power was transferred, I was closely involved at every step. We could discuss a wide range of topics—political, economic, etc.—without the fear of being misunderstood.

Since the days of the first president, Dr Rajendra Prasad, i.e., after 26 January 1950, the President of India lived in the Presidential House in the then guest wing, and converted the residential wing (more luxurious and well-decorated since the days of Lord Irving) as the guest wing. Therefore, all the invited chief guests would stay in Rashtrapati Bhavan, in addition to a number of dignitaries such as US President Dwight Eisenhower in 1959, UK's Queen Elizabeth II in 1983, when India hosted the Commonwealth Heads of Government Meeting, and the Saudi king, His Majesty Abdul Aziz Ibn Saud, in the winter of 1955. But somehow, this practice was given up in the mid-80s and the visiting heads of state to the capital were put up at starred, luxurious hotels.

In most places that I visited as president, including Sweden, Norway and Belgium, I was invited to live with the head of state in their official residence. However, I would decline politely on grounds of convenience and did not stay in their castles.

However, when I became president, I felt that we should create better facilities at Rashtrapati Bhavan, like those at the Kremlin, the White House and the Buckingham Palace. Looking at the size and the magnificent arrangements of the guest wing, I came to the conclusion that the wing could be better used if we allowed visiting heads of state or government and chief guests of the Republic Day to stay there.

Bhutan's royal couple were the first guests to stay at the refurbished Dwarka Suite (guest wing) of Rashtrapati Bhavan after two decades. Thereafter, a number of dignitaries stayed at Rashtrapati Bhavan, including PM Sheikh Hasina and Nepal's PMs, K.P.S. Oli and Pushpa Kamal Dahal.

FRIENDSHIP WITH JAPAN

Former Japanese PM Shinzo Abe had visited India several times. The decision to invite Abe as the chief guest at the Republic Day parade in 2014 was taken by PM Manmohan Singh. When he arrived in India, he came to Rashtrapati Bhavan straight from the airport and called on me (as president) on the evening of 25 January. He was accompanied by his wife, Akie Abe, and other senior officials. His delegation also included a number of top industrialists of Japan who were interested in further expanding business activities in India. I welcomed Abe to Rashtrapati Bhavan and reminded him that he was no stranger to India, as he had visited this country before and interacted with our senior leaders—the PM, the finance minister and other important leaders. I myself had met Abe just before he became PM for the first time. In my conversation with him, I reminded him that in his address to MPs at the Central Hall of Parliament during his visit in August 2007, he had mentioned that his grandfather, Nobusuke Kishi, the first Japanese PM ever to visit India, had held Nehru in high esteem. He had launched the post-war Official Development Assistance (ODA) in the early 50s and the first assistance was extended to India at that time. Since then, India had been the largest recipient of Japanese ODA in the world. Over the years, this has been enlarged to help infrastructure and new areas, such as forests, water management and other activities. In recent years, India has received Japanese ODA for key infrastructure projects, such as the Delhi Metro and the Western Dedicated Freight Corridor between Mumbai and Delhi. The Japanese government also provided upgradation assistance to improve the Chennai–Bengaluru industrial corridor.

In my conversation with Abe, I told him that before his arrival, I had the privilege of receiving His Majesty Emperor Akihito and his Queen in 2013, who visited India after 53 years. In fact, the Emperor and the Empress first visited India in the early 60s, immediately after their marriage, and spent quite some time visiting different parts of India. Abe mentioned my earlier visit to Japan as defence minister, and the interaction with him. During my visit in 2006, I had initiated defence cooperation with Japan; at that point in time, Japan was a bit reluctant to have any defence cooperation agreement and did not even have a defence ministry. The only security establishment it had was the institution of coast guard. Thereafter, Japan's defence minister would come to India to regularly discuss cooperation in wartime activities, particularly in ensuring the safety and security of the international trade route through the Malacca Straits, and our joint fight against the common menace of piracy. Abe maintained that he considered it a matter of privilege to be the chief guest at the Republic Day parade.

Abe's business delegation consisted of a large number of delegates. They had separate sessions with their counterparts, and later, both the PMs received a report of the meeting of the Indo-Japan Business Council.

In the summit meeting of September 2014, our strategic cooperation was upgraded to the level of a Strategic and Global Partnership. Abe's next visit to India as part of the bilateral annual summit meeting between the two PMs took place in September 2015. Abe also visited Varanasi to witness the famed Ganga Aarti at Dashashwamedh Ghat along with PM Modi.

The emergence of China, its ambition to be a superpower in the Asia-Pacific region and its relentless support to North Korea for its nuclear programme are matters of grave concern for Japan. In view of this prevailing geopolitical situation in the subcontinent, the India–Japan–US axis has become an important strategic group in the Asia-Pacific region.

The perception that India and Japan have become friends since the arrival of Modi as PM is not correct. We have had good relations with Japan even before 2014, and Abe had visited India before Modi became PM. As I mentioned earlier, the two countries had developed deep links in shared areas of activities and concerns. Abe's views on and rapport with Modi have been beneficial to India, though I do believe that personal friendships really do not matter in areas of national interest, which are driven by cold, hard facts.

I totally oppose the expressions of personal friendships (Abe called Modi his most dependable friend), because friendships are between countries. I do not subscribe to the belief that such special friendships have any worth when it comes to international relationships, where every relationship is impersonal. There are several instances from the past to support this fact. The best friendship prior to 1947 was perhaps between India and China; Zhou Enlai and Nehru were good friends. Several important Chinese leaders, who later fought and rebelled against those who wanted to establish the People's Republic, were Nehru's personal friends. In 1948, India was the only country to recognize the PRC after the Soviet Union. Then, we kept our national interests and not personal friendship in mind. But after Nehru's death in 1964, there was hardly any reference to this catastrophic event in Chinese newspapers. There was only one report that a condolence message was sent to the departed Indian leader's daughter, Indira Gandhi, on 27 May 1964. The Chinese have a peculiar way of expression.

Even my friendship with Bangladesh was completely political. Of course, my relationship with Sheikh Hasina was personal when she was in exile. Personally, I believe that PM Modi plays up personal equations too much. To take such relationships as true is a bit absurd.

UNDERSTANDING THE US

Barack Obama became the first US President to be invited as chief guest at the Republic Day parade in 2015, although most American presidents, since the days of Eisenhower, have visited India during their tenure. But not only was Obama the first exception as the chief guest for the Republic Day event, he is the only President of the US to have visited India twice during his tenure. The choice and presence of a chief guest for the Republic Day event does not convey any special message except to project friendship and proximity between the two countries; Obama's presence was no exception to this sentiment.

However, there was a difference in the protocol that was followed during the Republic Day parade that year. The normal practice is that the chief guest arrives at Rashtrapati Bhavan a few minutes before the president leaves the official residence for Rajpath, where the Republic Day parade takes place. Both the host and the guest share the same car while passing along the crowds before they arrive at the saluting dais. Before leaving Rashtrapati Bhavan, the president receives the national salute from the President's Bodyguard (PBG) and the guest watches the event. Then again the PBG gives the national salute to the president, which he takes from the dais, with the PM and other guests in presence. At the end of the function, the return journey is in the same order. From Rashtrapati Bhavan, the guest departs to his accommodation (in a hotel). In some cases, like with the King of Bhutan who stayed with the president, the guests accompanied me on both journeys.

In Obama's case, the US Secret Service insisted that their president travel in a specially armoured vehicle that had been brought along from the US. They wanted me to travel in the same armoured car along with Obama. This deviation raised a minor diplomatic issue. I politely but firmly refused to do so, and requested the MEA to inform the US authorities that when the US president travels with the Indian president in India, he would have to trust our security arrangements. It cannot be the other way around. So, ultimately, it was decided that Obama would come from his hotel in his car two minutes before my arrival and would be received by PM Modi; they would then receive me when I arrived. The same arrangement was made for my departure.

Incidentally, the parade of that year was tortuous for me because suddenly, in the midst of the parade, it began to rain heavily. There was a makeshift ceiling on the dais and all the guests were protected. In addition, a security guard stood holding an umbrella behind each guest. But for me, because of my height, a raised platform had been made, which was away from my seat, and was covered neither by a ceiling nor an umbrella. My distress was aggravated because I had both rainwater and water from the umbrella of an occupant near the chair, pouring on me. I was not physically very fit as I had come out of the hospital only three days before the parade, and doctors were concerned. Ultimately, one of my officials placed an overcoat and a Russian cap on me, and soon the rain stopped. Though my clothes were already wet, there was at least some comfort!

During the visit, Obama presented to me a facsimile of a telegram dispatched by former US president, Harry Truman, to our first president, Dr Rajendra Prasad, framed in a personalized plaque. It is preserved in a museum constructed during my time. This was followed by another personal gift in December 2015, when, as New Year greetings, Obama sent a card consisting of the signatures by everyone in the US first family along with the paw imprints of their two pets. This was true American humour, which has a personal touch of the guests. The overall impression that I had with my conversation with him was positive. I was impressed by the depth of his understanding of world affairs and also the developments in India since 1947.

During this visit, Obama said that I had, all through the decades—since the 70s till I became president, and through different phases of the India–US relationship—stood strongly in favour of promoting bilateral ties. He said that I had worked for it whether in office or out of it. I was totally taken aback, but I could do nothing. The newly appointed US envoy to India, Richard Verma, then told me that the president does not share his speech beforehand but speaks from the rostrum extempore.

However, regardless of the circumstances, as president, I always kept in mind that it was not my job to argue or impress upon my guests on the rationality of our views or our stand. As president, I only reiterated the stand taken and the views expressed by the government of the day. I never tried to be argumentative or to score a point.

CHAPTER 10

PATH-BREAKING DECISIONS: STORY OF DEMONETIZATION AND GST

The internal process of decision-making varies from government to government, and PM Modi has brought in a pattern where a major decision is endorsed by the cabinet or other appropriate bodies after the PMO or he himself has announced the decision. However, as per protocol, if it is a matter of policy, it is to be discussed in the cabinet, and naturally the finance minister takes the lead in initiating the discussions as desired by the PM. But in the last six years of this government, we have seen the introduction of new work procedures where most of the decisions are taken by the PMO in consultation with the departmental heads or secretaries concerned, as the case may be.

Of course, there are certain decisions that have to not only be taken at the PM's level but also have to be kept under wraps until their implementation. In other words, barring a select group of people led by the PM himself, nobody else is privy to the decision until its implementation at the shortest possible notice is announced. This is normally the case where an element of surprise is necessary to derive the best results. The Modi government's decision to demonetize, within a few hours of the announcement being made, high-value currencies, with a view to deal a body blow to the domestic black money economy, was one such instance. It has been both commended and criticized, although the jury is still out on whether it has achieved its main purpose.

PM Modi had not discussed the issue of demonetization with me prior to his announcement on 8 November 2016. I learnt of it along with the rest of the country when he made it known through a televised address to the nation. There has been criticism that he should have taken lawmakers and the Opposition into confidence, before making the announcement. I am of the firm opinion that demonetization could not have been done with prior consultation because the suddenness and surprise, absolutely necessary for such announcements, would have been lost after such a process.

Therefore, I was not surprised when he did not discuss the issue with me prior to making the public announcement. It also fitted in with his style of making dramatic announcements. According to reports, he spoke of it at a cabinet meeting and got the cabinet's consent just a short while before he went on air to tell the nation that high-value currency notes had been demonetized.

However, after delivering his address to the nation, the PM visited me at Rashtrapati Bhavan and explained to me the rationale behind his decision. Modi outlined three main objectives of demonetization: tackling black money, fighting corruption and containing terror funding. He desired an explicit support from me as a former finance minister of the country. I pointed out to him that while it was a bold step, it may lead to temporary slowdown of the economy. We would have to be extra careful to alleviate the suffering of the poor in the medium to long term. Since the announcement was made in a sudden and dramatic manner, I asked the PM if he had ensured that adequate currency was there for exchange.

Following the meeting, I issued a statement extending support to the principle of demonetization. I maintained that it was a bold step taken by the government that would help unearth unaccounted money as well as counterfeit currency. Incidentally, Bihar CM Nitish Kumar agreed to extend full support to the demonetization decision after I had endorsed it.

But demonetization wasn't an exercise initiated only by PM Modi. It had been discussed in Parliament and raised mainly by non-Congress parties several times, particularly from the 70s to the 90s. I remember in the early 70s, I had sent a note on demonetization to the PMO after the successful implementation of the Voluntary Disclosure of Income and Wealth Ordinance, 1975. A large amount of concealed income and wealth was declared by defaulters who stood in queues for long hours before officers of the Income Tax Department, in the last three days before the scheme was scheduled to close. It was regarded as the most successful one among several such schemes announced earlier by ministers like Mahavir Tyagi, T.T. Krishnamachari and Morarji Desai in the late 50s and 60s.

Indira Gandhi, however, did not accept my suggestion,

pointing out that a large part of the economy was not yet fully monetized and that a substantial part of it was in the informal sector. Under these circumstances, she argued, it would be imprudent to shake the faith of people in currency notes. After all, currency notes issued by the Reserve Bank of India (RBI) represent the commitment of a sovereign government. Except for the one-rupee note, which was signed by the finance secretary, all other currency notes above that value were, and are, signed by the RBI governor.

A similar sentiment seemed to have been echoed when, even after joining the European Economic Community—also known as the Common Market—the British government had not disturbed the faith of the citizens of its country, as well as international customers, in the currency notes issued by the sovereign government. In other words, lack of confidence in currency notes leads to lack of confidence in the credibility of the sovereign government.

Clearly, the problems associated with the demonetization policy were all well-known and the sufferings in the informal sector were also understandable. It was, therefore, natural for the decision to be questioned. Such decisions also shake the confidence of the people in the banking system. Former PM Manmohan Singh observed that as a result of demonetization, the impact on GDP growth would be at least 2 per cent negative growth—this has been established by the GDP growth numbers during the subsequent weeks of the government's dramatic decision. He used very strong words, describing it as 'organized loot and legalised plunder', with regard to the limitations of withdrawal of cash from the bank. The strong expression he used was because of the fact that genuine customers of the bank deposit money in good faith so that, in case of need, they would be able to withdraw the money. That facility had been denied in the immediate aftermath of the exercise.

Demonetization had been discussed in Parliament off and on for 17 years. And yet, when the announcement came, it brought with it a good amount of shock. Let us not forget that everyone is impacted by unaccounted cash in daily life, and unaccounted cash is amassed through the non-payment of taxes. Adequate measures were not taken to obviate the attendant problems that people faced. Further, large parts of the country continue to remain unmonetized and the practice of barter system continues in tribal areas. There is no doubt that demonetization and the consequential decisions of the government have had an adverse impact on the economy and GDP growth, resulting in an increase in unemployment in the medium term. The informal sector of the economy, which dealt with cash, was hurt severely.

However, it is difficult to assess the exact impact of demonetization, close to four years after it was implemented. But perhaps one thing can be stated without fear of contradiction: that the multiple objectives of the decision of demonetization, as stated by the government, to bring back black money, paralyse the operation of the black economy and facilitate a cashless society, etc., have not been met.

GOODS AND SERVICES TAX

The GST law is, in a way, the most effective economic legislation since the Constitution of India was enacted and operationalized. Its introduction was a momentous event for the nation.

The genesis of this path-breaking tax reform can be traced back to the year 2000 when PM Atal Bihari Vajpayee formed a committee to review the GST plan under the chairmanship of Asim Dasgupta, the then finance minister of West Bengal. The Kelkar Task Force on the implementation of the Fiscal Responsibility and Budget Management Act, 2003, had also suggested a comprehensive GST based on the value-added tax (VAT) principle.

Thereafter, the first concrete idea of GST came in the 2006 budget speech of P. Chidambaram in UPA-1. He referred the proposal to an Empowered Committee (EC) of State Finance Ministers chaired by Dasgupta, with a view to design a road map for the implementation of GST. In April 2008, the committee submitted its report to the central government, titled 'A Model and Road map for Goods and Services Tax (GST) in India', containing broad recommendations about the structure and design of GST. Hectic activity began thereafter to convert this idea into reality, though there was a period earlier when there was a complete standstill in the progress of GST.

Action was initiated in March 2009 (incidentally, I took over as the finance minister as an additional responsibility to my charge of external affairs), when the Department of Revenue made some suggestions to the design and structure of the GST. During my tenure as finance minister, I undertook the task to take forward the GST idea with strong determination. An attempt was made to develop a consensus for the passage of the bill by reactivating the functioning of a panel of state finance ministers, to be known as the GST Council, presided over by the union finance minister. To facilitate the constitutional requirement to have the competence to make the legislation, a Constitutional Amendment was passed with a majority and with the requisite number of state legislatures on board. A discussion paper was also drafted and circulated, and the discussions proceeded as per that discussion paper.

Based on the inputs from the Government of India and the states, the EC released its first discussion paper of GST on 10 November 2009, with the objective of generating a debate among all the stakeholders. Due to the political alignment, some of the states raised the issue of fiscal autonomy in the EC, through the finance ministers of Gujarat and Madhya Pradesh. That same year, in order to take the GST-related work further, a Joint Working Group consisting of representatives from the Union and the states was constituted. This was further trifurcated into three sub-working groups to concentrate separately on draft legislations that were needed for the GST, process and forms to be followed in the GST regime and the information technology (IT) infrastructure needed. The framework for the IT platform for GST implementation was laid under the chairmanship of Nandan Nilekani and a special purpose vehicle with cabinet approval was also set up.

There is no doubt that there had been a lack of political consensus on the constitutional amendments to provide the necessary legislative framework for GST. Some of the members of the EC were afraid of making changes to the existing structure. As a result, as finance minister, I had around 20 meetings with the CMs, and chairman and all members of the panel. Between

11 June 2009 and 17 April 2012, as many as 16 meetings were conducted by me with state finance ministers, members of the empowered panel, full panel (with me as chairman) and CMs. I visited Ahmedabad to meet the Gujarat CM; Patna, to meet the Bihar CM; Hyderabad, to discuss with the Andhra Pradesh CM; and also Mumbai, to deliberate with the Maharashtra CM. In fact, in 29 months, I held no less than 20 meetings.

Subsequent to these long-drawn and intensive discussions, in 2010, Chidambaram announced that the GST would be implemented from April 2011. After the budget speech of 2011–12, I had introduced the Constitution (115th Amendment) Bill, 2011 in the Lok Sabha in March 2011. The bill was then referred to a Parliamentary Standing Committee on Finance led by Yashwant Sinha, which submitted its report in August 2013.

Even though the parliamentary standing committee submitted its report to Parliament suggesting improvements on GST, and the bill was ready for introduction in Parliament in 2013, it didn't see the light of the day since the Lok Sabha was dissolved.

An observation of the then finance minister in his budget speech (the UPA's last budget speech) on GST in 2013 is extracted here:

> Honourable members will recall that I had first mentioned GST in the budget speech of 2007–08. At that point of time, it was thought that the GST could be brought into effect from 1 April 2010. Alas, that was not to be, although all states swear by the benefit of the GST. However, my recent meetings of the EC of State Finance Ministers has led me to believe that the state governments, or at least

the overwhelming majority, had agreed for the need of a constitutional amendment. There is need for state and central governments to pass a GST law that will be drafted by the state finance ministers and the GST Council and there is need for the Centre to compensate the states for loss due to the reduction in the GST rate.

The finance minister proposed a sum of ₹9,000 crore in his budget for the first instalment of the balances of the GST compensation. In my third budget after the introduction of the Constitution Amendment Bill in 2011–12, a sum of over ₹12,000 crore was provided in the budget estimate for the payment of state and union territory governments towards GST compensation.

The GST Bill, 2011, lapsed with the dissolution of the 15th Lok Sabha. The bill was further amended by Arun Jaitley, who served as finance minister when the BJP-led NDA came to power in 2014. Therefore, a fresh bill was introduced in the Lok Sabha in December 2014. Two years later, the Rajya Sabha endorsed it. As per the announcement of the then finance minister, Arun Jaitley, in the budget speech of 2015–16, the government intended to implement GST from the following year and envisaged putting in place a state-of-the-art indirect taxation by 1 April 2016.

As president, I gave my approval to the legislation in September 2016. Other developments took place thereafter—the GST Council was constituted, Assam became the first state to pass the GST law, Bihar became the first non-NDA-ruled state [the BJP then did not share power with the ruling JD(U)], the GST Network was formed, and eventually, the GST regime was launched from mid-July 2017.

When the GST Bill was passed by both the Houses and the GST was to be officially launched on 1 July 2017, it was decided to have a ceremonial session of both the Houses at midnight in the Central Hall of Parliament to formally adopt the bill in the presence of the cabinet, members of both the Houses, members of the diplomatic corps, state governors and CMs. PM Modi invited me to address the gathering on the midnight of 30 June. In fact, his phone call came early morning when I was taking my morning walk in the Mughal Gardens. Those were the days when I was getting ready to leave Rashtrapati Bhavan, as my term was coming to an end on 25 July 2017, with a new president (then yet to be declared as elected) was waiting to be sworn-in on that day. I informed the PM that I would speak with him after I return from my morning walk.

Coming back to my residence, I had a telephonic conversation with him, during which he insisted that as an individual, I had done my best for three-and-a-half years to get the bill passed, and as President of the Republic, the deal would be approved with my signature of assent. It would be a historic coincidence if I addressed the joint session of Parliament assembled at midnight at the Central Hall on 30 June. I agreed.

Officials from the department of revenue and Lok Sabha secretariat arrived and discussed the details of the programme with my office. That was my last ceremonial visit to Parliament, except for the farewell visit, when I was to retire from office.

I arrived in a ceremonial procession at gate number 5 of Parliament house, and was received by the vice president, speaker of the Lok Sabha, the PM and officers of both the Houses. The seating arrangement on the dais was different. The PM and the finance minister were seated on two sides. Finance Minister Jaitley made the introductory remarks, followed by the PM. Finally, before the stroke of the midnight hour, I made my observations.

I maintained that,

> GST is a disruptive change. It is similar to the introduction of VAT when there was initial resistance. When a change of this magnitude is undertaken, however positive it may be, there are bound to be some teething troubles and difficulties in the initial stages. We will have to solve these with understanding and speed to ensure that it does not impact the growth momentum of the economy. The success of such major changes always depends on their effective implementation. In the months to come, based on the experience of actual implementation, the GST Council and the central and state governments should continuously review the design and make improvements, in the same constructive spirit as has been displayed till now.

I expressed my deep appreciation for all those who had made tremendous efforts in making this path-breaking legislation. Thereafter, the bill was endorsed with a thumping of the tables. After a few minutes, I left the dais in a return ceremonial procession and came back to my official residence at Rashtrapati Bhavan.

Undoubtedly, the GST legislation has altered the Constitution very fundamentally because the financial resources of the Union of India vis-à-vis the states, as conceptualized by the framers of the Constitution, have been dealt with. In the Constitution, the activities of governments are placed in three categories. Subjects in the union list were the grounds of activity for federal legislation. Items in the state list in the Seventh Schedule were the playground of the state legislature. The third group of activity includes taxation on the concurrent list, by which both the Centre and the state governments have the authority to impose taxes. But the taxes imposed by the state governments under the concurrent list must be in tune with the central taxes.

The constitutional amendment to bring in the GST changed this structure. The constitutional boundaries of taxation limited to lists 1, 2 and 3 were blurred and even obliterated. Earlier, the central taxation authority was limited to central excise and customs in the areas of indirect taxes. State areas were sales tax, purchase tax, state excise duty, etc., The constitutional principle was that the Centre would not interfere with the state's authority and determine the taxes of sales, purchase, etc. and that the state regimes had no authority to encroach upon areas of central taxes. But with the new legislation, the union government has forfeited its right to impose central excise duty exclusively and the state governments have forfeited their rights of exclusivity to impose duty on sale and purchase. Now these rates have been brought under the GST Act, which will be concurrently formulated and operationalized by both the governments.

The GST regime is expected to play a transformative role in the way our economy functions. It will add buoyancy to the economy by developing a common Indian market and reducing the cascading effect on the cost of goods and services.

CHAPTER 11

MY PRIME MINISTERS: DIFFERENT STYLES, DIFFERENT TEMPERAMENTS

I have had the good fortune of interacting with and studying closely several PMs of India since Independence. They were different in mannerism, charisma, style and approach to governance. They came from different socio-economic backgrounds and some of them subscribed to widely distinct political ideologies. While it would be inappropriate to draw comparisons, their varied functioning does add to a deeper understanding of Indian politics.

Till date, India has had 15 PMs. A few of them had rather short terms—Charan Singh and Chandra Shekhar were PMs for less than a year. Morarji Desai (1977–79), V.P. Singh (1989–90), H.D. Deve Gowda and I.K. Gujral (both combined between 1996 and 1998) were some of the other PMs who had short tenures. Lal Bahadur Shastri, who became PM after Nehru's demise in 1964, had his tenure cut short when he died in 1966.

The longest tenure was that of the first PM, Jawaharlal Nehru, from 1947 to 1964—nearly 17 years. Indira Gandhi ruled as PM for over 15 years, in two spells during 1966–77 and 1980–84. Dr Manmohan Singh was PM for 10 consecutive years. All of these who served in the highest office for 10 years or more belonged to the Congress. Other Congress PMs such as Rajiv Gandhi and P.V. Narasimha Rao were in office for one five-year term. Some like Charan Singh, V.P. Singh and I.K. Gujral had earlier belonged to the Congress. Atal Bihari Vajpayee was the first BJP leader to become PM, and he was in office for six years (1998–2004). Narendra Modi, also from the BJP, took charge in mid-2014 and returned to power with a fresh public mandate in 2019.

Every PM has his or her own style of functioning. Lal Bahadur Shastri took positions that were very different from that of Nehru. There can be divergent perceptions among PMs, even if they happen to come from the same party, on issues such as foreign policy, security and internal administration. Nehru dealt with Nepal very diplomatically. After the Rana rule was replaced by the monarchy in Nepal, he wished for democracy to take root. Interestingly, Nepal's king, Tribhuvan Bir Bikram Shah, had suggested to Nehru that Nepal be made a province of India. But Nehru rejected the offer on the grounds that Nepal was an independent nation and must remain so. Had Indira Gandhi been in Nehru's place, she would have perhaps seized upon the opportunity, like she did with Sikkim. She was more assertive in building relationships with the Soviet Union. She showed her resolve in the midst of the 1971 war and the Bangladesh crisis.

In 1971, Mrs Gandhi, in her address to the General Assembly of the UN, mentioned that 84 Member States of the UN are so small that their combined population does not exceed 10 million in number. Now, if the internal policy of a sovereign country creates a situation in its own country where 10 million people are driven out of that country and compelled to take shelter in a neighbouring country, then how would these events be described in international law? Most humbly, I would like to know from the Members of the United Nations if this is not aggression then what else is the aggression of another country?

Incidentally, the same logic was advocated by a Soviet representative in the meeting of the UN Security Council to consider the resolution for issuing directives to effect immediate ceasefire by both India and Pakistan, while exercising veto on behalf of the Soviet Union. The representative pointed out that in this case the aggressor and aggressee are being treated equally. He elaborated that unless through a political solution, the basic problem of the people of East Pakistan—their demand to be governed by their own elected representatives—is not acceptable, how can this ceasefire proposal help bring back normalcy? In support of his observation, he quoted the views of Mrs Gandhi.

PRIME MINISTERS AND PRESIDENTS

From 26 January 1950 till date, India has seen the tenure of 14 presidents. V.V. Giri, Justice Mohammad Hidayatullah and B.D. Jatti—acted as president for the periods May–July 1969, July–August 1969 and February–July 1977, respectively. Of all the PMs, Nehru had to work with two presidents and two governor generals between August 1947 and May 1964.

In the initial days of the Republic, both President Rajendra

Prasad and PM Nehru established the norms of constitutional propriety in the relationship between the president and PM. It is something that has stood the nation in good stead to this day. During the later period, scholars and academia in pursuit of their research work have pointed out certain areas of difference between Nehru and Dr Prasad. But even if there were differences of opinion—and there had been quite a few—they were never manifested publicly during those days. There was no washing of dirty linen in public, and both the leaders handled contentious issues with dignity and maturity.

Indira Gandhi as PM worked with the highest number of presidents during her tenure of over 15 years, including Dr S. Radhakrishnan, who administered her the oath of office as PM in January 1966; then Zakir Hussain, V.V. Giri, Fakhruddin Ali Ahmed, B.D. Jatti (vice president acting as president), Neelam Sanjiva Reddy and Giani Zail Singh. The differences between Mrs Gandhi and Fakhruddin Ali Ahmed had been widely discussed while an inquiry commission under former CJI J.C. Shah went into the causes of declaring the internal Emergency in 1975, and the subsequent alleged abuse of constitutional powers and authority by the executive. But the controversy did not last long as the Shah Commission and its report on Emergency excesses were rejected by the government through a parliamentary resolution in the early 80s.

Even though Sanjiva Reddy and Mrs Gandhi belonged to opposite camps in the Congress, as president and PM they functioned smoothly within the constitutional framework, when she returned to power in 1980.

Then there were also reported differences between Giani

Zail Singh and Mrs Gandhi. The controversy between them on Operation Blue Star (in which the Indian Army, under orders from the Centre, stormed the sacred Golden Temple in Amritsar to flush out militant terrorist leader Jarnail Singh Bhindranwale and his men) has not yet been well-researched and substantially established. It remained in the realm of rumour and died so. It is a fact, though, that Singh had been close to Mrs Gandhi as one of her ministers, before he was elevated to the high position of head of the state.

Many years later, there were occasional reports of differences of opinion between President K.R. Narayanan and PM Atal Bihari Vajpayee, but the seriousness of those so-called differences is yet to be firmly established through documented research.

On the other hand, relations between PM Manmohan Singh and President Pratibha Patil were absolutely smooth. We did not hear of any differences between them during her tenure in 2007–12. But I remember that Dr Singh once asked me to meet her and explain the constitutional role to her clearly, even in the functioning of Parliament. He did not elaborate. I sought an appointment with the President and she immediately invited me over for lunch. She said that she was distressed over the frequent parliamentary disruptions and deadlock in transacting business in the House. I explained to her that as the leader of the House in the Lok Sabha and a member of the cabinet, I fully shared her concerns. I also added that while occasionally Parliament erupts on certain issues, over the years we have developed a system through which such emotional upsurges are finally tackled and resolved. I reported to the PM the discussions I had had with the President. There was no further action and the matter rested there.

During my own presidency, I had the opportunity to work with two PMs—Dr Singh (from 25 July 2012 to 26 May 2014), almost two years in the first half of my five-year tenure; and then, from 26 May till the day of my retirement from the office on 25 July 2017, I had Narendra Modi as my PM, for a little more than three years.

The route to prime ministership for the two PMs I worked with was very different. Dr Singh was offered the post by Sonia Gandhi; she had been chosen as the prime ministerial candidate by the Congress Parliamentary Party and other constituents of the UPA, but she declined the offer. The issue of her foreign origin was being heatedly debated in the public domain, and she did not want to create a controversy as a result of the division that had been created out of the matter. Senior leaders such as Sharad Pawar, P.A. Sangma and Tariq Anwar had in 1999 insisted that the Congress name an Indian by birth as its prime ministerial candidate and not someone like Sonia Gandhi, who was of foreign origin and had become the party chief. They were expelled and went on to form the NCP.

Once the Congress realized that Sonia Gandhi would not relent, it authorized her to name a candidate. She named Dr Singh and others accepted her choice. He was essentially an economist, though he had spent time in government as a minister and in politics as a Rajya Sabha member. But he had determination and a strong sense of propriety. He had a steely willpower, which he demonstrated during the civil nuclear deal that India finalized with the US, despite opposition from various quarters, including certain parties that supported the government from outside. He did well as a PM.

Modi, on the other hand, became PM through popular choice after leading the BJP to a historic victory in 2014. He is a politician to the core and had been named the BJP's prime ministerial candidate as the party went into campaign mode. He was then Gujarat's CM and had built an image that seemed to click with the masses. He has earned and achieved the prime ministership.

COPYBOOK RELATIONSHIPS

I had already had a long working relationship with Dr Singh since the mid-70s. When I was appointed minister of state for revenue and expenditure in the Ministry of Finance in 1974, Dr Singh was chief economic advisor to the finance minister. In 1982, when I took over as the union minister for finance, he was appointed governor of the RBI.

Again, in 1991, when Dr Singh was appointed the finance minister, I was the deputy chairman of the Planning Commission, and while formulating the eighth FYP, I received the utmost cooperation and support from him. From 1993 onwards, when I concurrently discharged the responsibility of commerce minister, we worked together in expanding India's international trade. He was one of the cabinet ministers who fully endorsed my approach to establish the WTO after the Marrakesh Declaration of 1994. Later on, both of us worked closely in the Rajya Sabha as he was leader of Opposition and I was the chief whip of the Congress party. Again, from 2004 onwards, I joined his cabinet, first as defence minister, then as external affairs minister, and finally as finance minister, till 25 June 2012, when I resigned to contest the office of president.

With this long working relationship spanning over five decades from 1970, I had an excellent sense of understanding with Dr Singh, and I believed both of us knew each other so well that there was no scope of any misunderstanding between us as president and PM. Moreover, when I agreed to accept the nomination of the Congress-led UPA as the presidential candidate and was elected by an overwhelming majority, I knew that my active political role had come to an end and that I would have to conduct myself as a constitutional head and not interfere unnecessarily in the domain of the executive. I had done enough of executive work for decades and now it was time to step back and adhere to the constitutional role that a president is expected to perform.

I had resolved to never cross the limits that my new position imposed on me. I had a clear understanding of the constraints of holding this highest constitutional office and had convinced myself that, as president, I was not supposed to intervene in the day-to-day matters of the executive, since the cabinet, and the cabinet alone, is responsible for that. The president has the right to know and to be informed. It is not his job to mentor anybody. Perhaps this understanding of constitutional propriety helped me have a smooth sailing as the 13th President of the Republic.

However, on one occasion I questioned the PM on an ordinance his government proposed to bring. The recommendation for the ordinance came to my office accompanied by a note from the member in charge (or the relevant minister). I called for an explanation from the said minister. He had in Parliament sought to refer the issue, on which the ordinance was routed to me, to a parliamentary panel for further discussion. I wanted to know

On a solid pitch: The PM of Australia, Julia Gillard, on a visit to New Delhi in 2012.

A dynamic relationship rooted in deep people-to-people ties: The PM of Canada, Stephen Harper, on a visit to India in 2012.

Meeting the PM of Bhutan, Lyonchhen Tshering Tobgay, and his spouse, Aum Tashi Doma, in 2013, on their first overseas visit after the PM's election.

With the PM of Iraq, Nouri al-Maliki, in 2013.

With the PM of Hungary, Viktor Orban, in 2013.

Presenting a coffee table book to UK PM David Cameron at Rashtrapati Bhavan in 2013.

Showcasing our cultural diversity: Welcoming Charles, Prince of Wales, and his wife, Camilla, Duchess of Cornwall, in 2013.

Creating history: Meeting the PM of Pakistan, Nawaz Sharif, in 2014. His attendance at PM Modi's swearing-in ceremony was a first in the history of the two countries.

Welcoming a deeply valued friend: With the PM of Sri Lanka, Ranil Wickremesinghe, and his spouse, (Prof.) Maithree Wickramasinghe, in 2015.

Greeting UN Secretary General, Ban Ki-moon, in 2015, who described India as having 'a very special place in his heart'.

Partnership for prosperity: Meeting the PM of Japan, Shinzo Abe, in 2015.

The PM of Nepal, Pushpa Kamal Dahal 'Prachanda', pays a courtesy call at Rashtrapati Bhavan in 2016.

Shared democratic values and a Commonwealth heritage: With the PM of New Zealand, John Key, in 2016.

The visit of Ruhakana Rugunda, the PM of Uganda, in 2017, exemplified the new spirit of cooperation with Africa.

the urgency of issuing the proclamation, especially when the member in charge as the author himself did not believe the issue was urgent, since he had wanted it referred to a committee. I have always held that an ordinance should only be issued in emergency cases when a legislation cannot be delayed any further. Sensing my disquiet, the PM spoke to his minister, who then informed me that the government had decided to withdraw the ordinance. The matter ended there.

My approach to maintaining cordial relations with PM Modi was rooted in the fact that I believe in the parliamentary form of government and its principle. Modi had received a decisive mandate from the people to administer the country. Administrative powers are vested in the Council of Ministers, which the PM heads. Therefore, I did not breach my jurisdiction. Whenever tricky occasions arose, the issues were resolved. At an event in which PM Modi released a book and I was present, I remarked that it was not that I did not have any differences with him, but that both of us knew how to manage those differences, without bringing them out in public.

As I look back, I can take satisfaction over my performance both as president and earlier as a member of the executive. At all times I have followed the law of the land and held the Constitution supreme. Looking ahead, I believe that the country is firmly on the path of progress despite the many challenges that it faces. We must, however, not allow complacence to set in and endanger the gains that we have had because of the relentless efforts of the founders of our independent nation and the framers of our Constitution.

EPILOGUE

When I look back on my years as president, I derive satisfaction not only from the fact that I followed the rule book in letter and spirit in dealing with governments and issues of the day, but also because I never veered from the constitutional parameters that have been laid down for an Indian head of state. The satisfaction is also from the realization that I took several initiatives to expand the scope of activities within Rashtrapati Bhavan and the larger President's Estate, most of which yielded tangible results during my tenure. More importantly, they have continued even after I completed my tenure and slipped into the life of a private citizen. I do not look at these achievements in terms of my legacy, because 'legacy' is too exalted an expression and embarrasses me. Nonetheless, they are matters of pride for me.

In the first year of my presidency, I made it a point to visit as many parts of the country as possible—I covered 23 states and union territories, including J&K and parts of the North-East, addressed various state legislative assemblies and spoke on the need to avoid disruptions in House proceedings and legislation through the ordinance routes. I addressed various courts and other legal institutions and highlighted issues of speedy justice, judicial accountability and alternative methods of dispute resolution, encouraged Indian and foreign investors to shun gloom and take heart from the sound fundamentals of the Indian economy, and met various foreign envoys in India and abroad with a view to strengthening Indian diplomacy.

However, the various measures I took to make Rashtrapati Bhavan accessible to the common man have given me real happiness. One, Rashtrapati Bhavan was thrown open to ordinary citizens three days a week, through an online booking mechanism. Two, the visitors' reception hall was revamped to make it more people-friendly, with special furniture gathered from various parts of the country. Three, trained guides and scholar guides were deployed to take the visitors on a tour of the place and educate them on its history and ethos. Four, cultural programmes were organized once a month in Rashtrapati Bhavan auditorium, for which members of the public and students were invited. A number of nationally and internationally renowned artists such as Pandit Hariprasad Chaurasia, Shubha Mudgal, the Warsi brothers, Girija Devi, Aruna Sairam and Shekhar Sen performed at these events, thus bringing the musical and cultural flavour of this diverse country to life. The Ao Naga Choir, Shriram Bharatiya Kala Kendra and Turkish Dervishes mesmerized audiences with their performances. Five, an internship programme was conducted at Rashtrapati Bhavan to offer an opportunity to students to learn more about the Bhavan's functioning. Apart from these, many other initiatives were also taken.

I strongly believe that Indians must have a sense of their history. In keeping with my desire to recreate the past—not to cling to it but to generate awareness of history—I revived, after a gap of almost three decades, the tradition of using the buggy (horse-drawn carriage) for ceremonial events such as the Beating Retreat.

I took a keen interest in the restoration of Rashtrapati Bhavan Library, bringing together old and rare books dating from 1795 CE into the main library room. An audio-visual section was added to the library, which contained recordings of speeches of luminaries, including Rajendra Prasad, C. Rajagopalachari and Lord Mountbatten. Rare and invaluable books that were in poor shape were restored with the help of experts from the Indira Gandhi National Centre for the Arts (IGNCA).

I also instructed that a comprehensive conservation management plan be prepared to serve as a blueprint for all future constructions, so that the President's Estate could be restored to its plan as originally outlined by Sir Edwin Lutyens and others who had conceptualized the estate. The Indian National Trust for Art and Cultural Heritage was taken on board as a consultant for the project. Once the report came in, work on the project began in right earnest.

During my second year in office, I continued with my determination to connect Rashtrapati Bhavan with the common man. An innovative programme was launched to provide residency in the Bhavan to writers and artists, selected through a national-level screening process, to conduct research. I recall with pleasure that one of the selected candidates happened to be a rickshaw-puller before he took to being a research scholar. It was a matter of deep satisfaction for me that over 60 lakh people visited Rashtrapati Bhavan during the second year of my presidency.

My third year in office saw the flourishing of the in-residence programme, the number of visitors to the Bhavan continued to be impressive and the first-ever museum was inaugurated at Rashtrapati Bhavan. Besides, I took interest in the various welfare measures to improve the lives of nearly 7,000 residents of Rashtrapati Bhavan. The Bhavan was declared a Financially Inclusive Township, with Internet connectivity, etc.

In continuation of my efforts, in my fourth year in office, the President's Estate was recast as a 'Humane, Hi-tech, Heritage and Happy Township' in the fourth year of my tenure. Besides, five villages of Haryana were adopted by Rashtrapati Bhavan to make them model 'Smart Grams'. On Teacher's Day, I donned the garb of a tutor and addressed a gathering of 113 heads of institutions of higher learning from across the country. The first-ever international conference of Indologists, attended by representatives of various nations, was also organized. These initiatives gave me an opportunity to not just share my thoughts with people but also learn from the experts.

Steps were taken to involve and benefit citizens, from children to the aged. The Pranab Mukherjee Public Library organized the 'Sanskriti' programme under which yoga, painting, clay modelling, music and storytelling classes were held for children. 'Samagam' for senior citizens and 'Sparsh' for specially abled were also held.

My final year in office saw further improvements in facilities at Rashtrapati Bhavan and the President's Estate in general. Rainwater harvesting techniques were put in place for residential quarters of the staff. Besides, energy-efficient lighting systems, recycling of waste-water and solar water-heating arrangements were made. Steps were also taken to promote defensive (safe) driving and respect for traffic rules. This programme for residents of the President's Estate was conducted with the assistance of the Driver Training Institute, Burari. A grand yoga camp was also organized, with yoga guru Baba Ramdev participating in it. The President's Estate Clinic was modernized with the addition of latest computerized equipment in its various departments. Visiting doctors, with specialized skills, were called to offer guidance to patients. Alternative systems of medicine such as Ayurveda and Unani, as well as holistic treatments such as neuropathy, acupuncture, acupressure and clinical psychology, proved to be immensely helpful to patients from the President's Estate.

During my tenure, the publication of a multi-volume project to highlight various features related to Rashtrapati Bhavan—architecture, archaeological significance, paintings and other artefacts—was undertaken. It was done with the collaboration of the IGNCA and Sahapedia. One of the volumes brought out the various architectural aspects of this historical building. The chapters were written by eminent architects and historians, and the guiding force was provided by eminent landscape architect, Mohammad Shaheer. He was associated with the project until the penultimate stage; his sudden demise in November 2015 left us shocked.

A volume detailing the history and origins of the President's bodyguards was published too. Titled, *Right of the Line: The President's Bodyguard*, it detailed the 240-year-old tradition of the regiment and its modern-day role. Another volume presented the transformation of the Rashtrapati Bhavan into a knowledge hub, with the introduction of various activities and programmes to spread modern and traditional knowledge.

It has been a matter of great satisfaction to me that these volumes will serve experts, the academia and the common man for decades to come and lead to a greater understanding and appreciation of the institution that is Rashtrapati Bhavan.

For me, it is a matter of pleasure that the many steps taken during my tenure in several areas continue to make life better and more meaningful for both Rashtrapati Bhavan and the residents of the President's Estate. I consider this achievement to be no less satisfying than the other duties I performed as head of state to keep the Indian flag flying high.

INDEX

Abbas, Mahmoud, 133
Abe, Akie, 148
Abe, Shinzo, 148
Absentee leadership, 8–10
   physical presence of the PM in Parliament, 9
Address to parliament, 35–38
   budget session (2015), 35
   joint session of parliament (2017), 37
Adhikari, Manmohan, 100
Advani, L.K., 23, 39
Afghan-India Friendship Dam, 111
Afghanistan, 111–12
   bond with, 111
   building of Afghanistan's Parliament by India, 111
   instability in, 21
   internal tribal wars, 111
   rebuilding of the Habibia High School in Kabul, 111
   reconstruction of the Salma dam, 111
   restoration of the Stor Palace, 111
   SAARC membership, 111–12
   training to Afghan police and military personnel, 111
   US intervention to coutner Taliban, 111
Africa, 112–13
AFRICA outreach, 112
Agrarian Relations Bill, 53
Ahmed, Fakhruddin Ali, 170
Aishwarya, Queen, 101
All India Anna Dravida Munnetra Kazhagam (AIADMK), 106
Alva, Joachim, 38
Ambedkar, B.R., 47–48
Anwar, Tariq, 172
Appropriation Bill, 57
Article 352 of Constitution, use of, 50
Article 356 of Constitution, 44, 49–51, 53–54, 57, 59–60
   abolition of, 52
   contentious provisions, 44
   debate on the use and misuse of, 53
   neutral, neither positive nor negative, 60
   opposed the abolition of, 52
   presidential proclamations arising out of, 54
   stand on, 50

use of, 59
See also Constitution
Asian Infrastructure and Investment
   Bank, 99
Association of Southeast Asian Nations
   (ASEAN), 140
Awami League, 116
Azad, Ghulam Nabi, 11
Azhar, Maulana Masood, 138

Balochistan, 115
Bandaranaike, Sirimavo, 105
Bandaranaike, Solomon, 105
Banerjee, Mamata, 20, 116, 120
Bangabandhu Memorial Museum, 120
Bangla Academy, 120
Bangla Sahitya Sammelan, 120
Bangladesh Muktijuddho Sanmanona
   (Liberation War award), 119
Bangladesh Nationalist Party, 118
Bangladesh
   fondness for, 115
   personal relationship with PM
      Sheikh Hasina, 115
Bara massacre, 79–80
Baruah, Golap (Anup Chetia), 115
Baruah, Paresh, 115
Battle of Plassey, 32
Bharatiya Jana Sangh, 17
Bharatiya Janata Party (BJP), 5, 16–19,
   22–24, 29, 54, 57, 76, 94, 163, 168,
   173
   as a component of the Janata Party,
      17
   National Democratic Alliance
      (NDA), 5, 8, 18, 163
   onslaught under Modi's leadership,
      18
   performance in earlier elections, 17
Bhindranwale, Jarnail Singh, 171

Bhutan
   concept of common security with,
      146
   rise of nascent democracy in, 21
Bhutto, Zulfikar Ali, 87
Bikram Shah, Tribhuvan Bir, 168
Birendra, King, 100–1
Blackstonian theory, 68
BRICS, 99
British East India Company, 45
Budget session, 3–4, 35

Capital punishment, 72, 77–82, 88
   abolition of, 81–82. *See also* Mercy
      petition, 81
   moratorium on an end of, 81
Catholic Church, 53
Centre-state relations, critical nature
   of, 47
Chagla, M.C., 38
Chandra Shekhar, 167
Chaturvedi, Satyavrat, 11
Chaurasia, Hariprasad, 178
Chelameswar, J., 67
   raised doubts over collegium system,
      67
Chief Justice, swearing-in ceremony
   of, 69
Chidambaram, P., 77, 160, 162
   in UPA-1, 160
China, 96, 137–40
   border dispute, 139
   cultural exchange and institutional
      arrangements, 138
   'Dalai clique', 137–38
   growing influence in Nepal, 104
   issue of Maulana Masood Azhar,
      138–39
   McMahon Line, 139
   people-to-people contacts, 138

trade and investment in early 90s, 137
Chittagong Armoury Raid, 121
Choir, Ao Naga, 178
Citizen-friendly governance, 33
Civil nuclear agreement, 93
Clean India mission, 37
Climate change, 41
Coalition governments, 19, 22
Cold War, 83, 93, 132
   end of, 93, 132
Collegium system, 65–67, 70
   doubts over, 67
   establishment of, 70
   favour of the, 66
   proponents of the, 66
   responsibility of, 71
   See also Judiciary
Commission of Inquiry Act, 7
Common Market. See European Economic Community
Common Minimum Programme, 19
Commonwealth Heads of Government Meet (CHOGM), 136
Communist Party of India (Maoist), 79
Competitive federalism, 48
Comprehensive Nuclear-Test-Ban Treaty (CTBT), 92
Congress Parliamentary Party, 172
Congress
   disqualification to the rebel, 58
   disruptive agenda, 5
   failed fulfil people's expectations and aspirations, 17
   strong anti-Eelam policy, 108
   worst defeat in 30 years, 18
   led UPA, 5, 14, 174
Constitutional Amendments
   42nd Amendment, 12, 49–52. See also Emergency

44th Amendment, 49–51, 59
115th Amendment Bill, 2011, 162
Amendment Bill, introduction of the, 163
parliament's right to amend, 68
Constitutional division, 62–63
Constitutional parameters, 177
Constitutional responsibility, 22
Cooperative federalism, 35, 48
Creative thinking, innovation and scientific temper, 42
Cultural programmes, 178

Dahal, Pushpa Kamal 'Prachanda', 101, 148
Dalai Lama, 96, 137–38
Dalhousie, Lord, 45
Das, C.R., 8
Dasgupta, Asim, 160
Dattu, H.L., 69
Decision-making, internal process of, 155
Defence Framework Agreement, 93–94
Democratic instrument, 26
Demonetization, 155–59
   consequential decisions, 159
   difficult to assess the exact impact of, 159
   discussed in Parliament, 157, 159
   main objectives of, 156–57
   principle of, 157
   problems associated, 158
Desai, Morarji, 6, 50, 157, 167
Deshmukh, Vilasrao, 21
Development-oriented politics, 16
Devi, Girija, 178
Dharam Vira case, 57–58
Digital India, 37
Direct Benefit Transfer programme, 35
Distinguished Indologist award, 134

Doctrine of Lapse, 45–46
Doctrine of the Constitution, basic structure, 68
Doklam stand-off, 130
Double Taxation Avoidance Treaty (DTAA), 121–22
   interpretation of certain clauses, 122
Dravida Munnetra Kazhagam (DMK), 20, 106–8

East Asia Summit, 99
East India Company, 45–46
Economic growth rate, 32
Education, 37, 41–42, 103, 132–33, 136, 138
Education Bill, 53
Eisenhower, Dwight, 147
'Either-Israel-or-Palestine scenario', 135
Election Commission, 21
Electoral malpractices, 11
Electronic voting machines (EVMs), irregularities in, 11
Emergency, 18, 38, 49–51, 105, 170
Enlai, Zhou, 151
Environmental protection, 41
European Economic Community, 158
Eurozone crisis, 32

Farewell speech, 38–43
   declining number of days Parliament, 39
   education system, 42
   important issues in, 39
   mix of nostalgia and present-day realities, 38
   tributes to Indira Gandhi, 38
Federal structure, 45–49
'Federation of India', establishment of a, 46
Final address to the nation, 40

Financial Action Task Force (FATF), 95
   Pakistan' was placed on the watch-list, 95
Finland, Nokia, 128
Finland, supply of paper pulp, 126–28
First War of Independence. *See* Sepoy Mutiny (1857 revolt)
Fiscal Responsibility and Budget Management Act, 2003, 160
Five-Year Plans (FYPs), 36, 130, 145, 173
Foreign policy, 83–113
   Africa outreach, 112–13
   bond with Afghanistan, 111–12
   dealing with Pakistan, 86–91
   friendship with Nepal, 99–105
   India–China partnership, 84, 96–99
   India–US ties, 91–96
   relations with Maldives, 110
   relations with the major powers, 83
   relationship with Russia, 84
   working with Sri Lanka, 105–10
Foreign visits, 114–42
   African countries, 140–41
   Bangladesh, 118–21
   Belgium, 89, 123–24
   Bhutan, 130–31
   China, 137–40
   Finland, 126
   Helsinki address, 126–27
   Israel, 135
   Mauritius, 121–23
   New Zealand, 136
   Norway, 126
   Palestine, 135
   Papua New Guinea, 136
   Russia, 131–35
   South Africa, 140
   Sweden, 128–29
   Turkey, 123–24

Vietnam, 124–25
Friendship with Japan, 148–51
   Abe visit to see Ganga Aarti at Dashashwamedh Ghat, 150
   Official Development Assistance (ODA), 149
   strategic cooperation upgraded, 150
   upgradation assistance to improve the Chennai–Bengaluru industrial corridor, 149
Friendship with Nepal, 99–105
   complex character of India-Nepal relationship, 104
   contribution by India in development of Nepal, 103
   India–Nepal Treaty of Peace and Friendship, 100
   Maoist insurgency, 101
   people-to-people relationship, 99
   political developments in Nepal, 99
   political ups and downs in Nepal, 103
   relief and rehabilitation package in 2015 earthquake, 104
   See also Foreign policy
Fundamental rights of citizens, 50

G20, 99
Gandhi, Indira, 9, 15, 38, 49, 58, 60, 92, 105, 129, 141, 151, 157, 167–171
   7th NAM summit, 141
   assassination, 15, 58
   differences with Fakhruddin Ali Ahmed, 170
   discussion of demonetization with, 157–58
   Emergency, 49, 105
   made presence felt on the floor of the House, 9
   as PM worked with the highest
   number of presidents, 170
   returned to power in 1980, 60
   ruled as PM for over 15 years, 167–68
   tributes to Indira Gandhi in farewell speech, 38
   UN General Assembly address (1971), 168
Gandhi, Mahatma, 8, 128–29
   relevance of, 128
   votary of peace, 129
Gandhi, Rahul, 11, 13
Gandhi, Rajiv, 15, 58, 82, 106–8, 136, 168
   assassination, 107
   attacked by a Sri Lankan army man, 107
   victim of a terror attack, 106
Gandhi, Sonia, 11, 13, 20–21, 172
   decisions taken by, 21
   unable to handle the affairs of the party, 20
Ganga Aarti at Dashashwamedh Ghat, 150
Ganga Water Sharing Treaty of 1996, 116
Geelani, S.A.R., 76
General elections (2014), 15–24
   BJP emerged with a simple majority, 16
   Congress managed to win just 44 seats, 23
   decisive mandate, 15
   invitation all the heads of SAARC countries, 24
   mandate in favour of PM Modi, 17
   meeting the PM-Designate (Narendra Modi), 23–24
   swearing-in ceremony, 24
Ghosh, Rash Behari, 8

Giri, V.V., 169–70
Golaknath case, 67
Golden Temple, 171
Goods and Services Tax, 11, 34, 155, 159–66
  constitutional amendment to bring, 34, 166
  design and structure of, 160
  disruptive change, 165
  expected to play a transformative role, 166
  first concrete idea, 160
  first discussion paper, 161
  GST Bill, 163–64
  GST compensation, 163
  GST Council, 160–61, 163, 165
  GST legislation, 165
  platform for implementation, 161
  legislative framework for, 161
  officially launched 1 July 2017, 164
  political alignment, 161
  road map for 160
  tax reform, 160
  UPA's last budget speech on GST, 162
Goodwill gestures, 123
Government of India Act, 1935, 46–47
Gowda, H.D. Deve, 25, 115, 167
Goyal, Piyush, 17
Gujral, I.K., 108, 115, 167–68
  dependent on the DMK for survival, 108
Gupta, Bhupesh, 38
Guru, Afzal, 76–77, 80
  capital punishment ot, 77
  confessional statement, 76
Gyanendra, King, 101–2

Hamid, Abdul, 118, 121
Harrod-Domar Model, 36

Hasina, Sheikh, 115–21, 148, 151
Hazare, Anna, 9. *See also* Lokpal Bill
Hidayatullah, Justice Mohammad, 169
Historic visits, 131–36
  Israel, 135–36
  New Zealand, 136
  Palestine, 135–36
  Papua New Guinea, 136
  Russia, 131–35
  See also Foreign visits; Indo-Russian relationship
How India Sees the World, 102
'Humane, Hi-tech, Heritage and Happy Township, 180
Hussain, Zakir, 170

Independence Day addresses, 28
India–Africa Forum Summit (IAFS), 112
India–Bangladesh matters, 115
India–China partnership, 95–99
  asylum to the Dalai Lama, 96
  bilateral trade, 97
  border dispute, 139
  China's Belt and Road Initiative, 98
  Chinese waiver to entering the Nuclear Suppliers Group (NSG), 97
  Doklam standoff (2017), 98
  peace and tranquility along the Line of Actual Control, 97
  Shangri-La Dialogue, 96
  ups and downs, 97
  See also Foreign policy
Indian Council Act of 1892, 7
Indian Council for Cultural Relations (ICCR), 97, 134
India-Nepal Treaty of Peace and Friendship, 100
Indian National Trust for Art and

Cultural Heritage, 179
Indian Penal Code (IPC), 76, 81–82
Indian Union Muslim League, 19
India–US–China triangle, 95
India–Vietnam relationship, 125
Indira Gandhi National Centre for the Arts (IGNCA), 179
Indo-African trade relations, 112
Indo-Bangladesh relation, 116–20
  land boundary agreement, 117
  relationship with, 114
    Teesta water-sharing dispute, 116–18, 120–21
Indo-Bhutan Friendship Treaty, 145
Indo-Finnish Joint Commission, 127
Indo-Japan Business Council, 150
Indo-Pak relations
  26/11 terror attacks, 90
  Army's dominance in Pakistan, 89
  creation of a Bangladesh, 87
  equality concept, 87
  failed armed intervention by Pakistan (1965), 87
  war of 1971, 87, 91
  Imran Khan's emergence as PM, 89
  negative thoughts, 86
  Pathankot terrorist attack, 88–89
  policy of aggression, 86
  Tashkent Declaration, 87
  terrorism fostered by the religious fundamentalists, 88
  tribal invasion into Kashmir (1947), 87
  unfinished agenda of Partition, 87
Indo-Russian relationship, 131–35
  balance of power, 132
  detailed discussions with Putin on aspects ranging from civil nuclear, 131
  educational cooperation, 133

engagement between educational institutions, 134
'Namaste Russia' festival, 133
Rupee-Rouble Agreement, 134
Indo-Sri Lanka Free Trade Agreement, 106
Indo-US relationship, 93–94, 154
  aggressive American policies, 92
  American attitude of looking through the Pakistan prism, 91
  areas of conflict, 94
  civil nuclear agreement with the US (2008), 93
  CTBT Treaty, 92
  Defence Framework Agreement, 93–94
  economic policies, 92
  linguistic heritage, 91
  NPT Treaty, 92
  phases of, 154
  PM Modi's efforts to improve relations, 94–95
  support from US through PL 480, a Food for Peace initiative, 93
  US approach during liberation movement of Bangladesh, 91
  See also Foreign policy
Information technology (IT) infrastructure, 161
institutionalized disruptions, system of, 3
International Yoga Day, 37
Intra-party rivalries, 18
Inu, Hasanul Haq, 120

Jaishankar, S., 139
Jaitley, Arun, 23, 58, 163–64
Jamaat-i-Islami, 118
Jana Sangh, 17–19
  closely linked with the RSS, 19

Janata Dal (United) [JD(U)], 20
Janata Party, 17–19, 50, 59
Jatti, B.D., 169–70
Jawaharlal Nehru University (JNU), 76
Jayawardene, J.R., 105
Jharkhand Mukti Morcha, 20
Jiechi, Yang, 139
Jinping, Xi, 139
Jintao, Hu, 97
Joint Intelligence Team (JIT), 88
Joshi, Murli Manohar, 23
'Judicial activism', 63. *See also* Judiciary
Judiciary, 61–71
   achieving balance, 68–71
   collegium, 65–67, 70–71
   Constitutional framework, 62
   executive, legislature and, 61
   expenditure on, 69
   funds requirement for expansion, 69
   hyperactive, 62
   impeachment process to remove judges, 64
   intervention of, 63
   judicial appointments, 65–68
   mandate out of overenthusiasm, 63
   oversee the implementation of laws, 62
   power of interpretation, 62
   responsible organ of democracy, 64
   role, 61, 68
   selection and appointment of judges, 65
Jugnauth, Anerood, 121
Jury system, 80–81
Justice delivery system, 69

Kabir, Altamas, 69
Kadirgamar, Lakshman, 108
Kai-shek, Chiang, 92, 95
Kalam, A.P.J. Abdul, 43, 73

Kapadia, S.H., CJI, ix, 69
Karmakar, Deepa, 37
Karunanidhi, M., 108
Kasab, Ajmal, 75, 78, 80
   mercy plea, 75
Kejriwal, Arvind, 13
Kelkar Task Force, 160
Keshavananda Bharati vs. State of Kerala case (1973), 67–68
Khalistan agitation, 52
Khan, General Ayub, 87, 89
Khan, Imran, 89–90
Khan, Yahya, 89
Khanna, H.R., 68
Khehar, J.S., 66, 69
Kishi, Nobusuke, 149
Kovind, Ram Nath, 113
Krishnamachari, T.T., 157
Kumar, Nitish, 157
Kumar, Ranjit, 78
Kumaratunga, Chandrika, 107
Kumaratunga, Vijaya, 107

Lakshmibai of Jhansi, Queen, 46
Land Boundary Agreement, 117
Last ceremonial visit to Parliament, 164
Law Commission, 81
Leadership in times of crisis, 20–21
Left-wing extremism, 37
Liberation movement of Bangladesh, 91
Liberation Tigers of Tamil Eelam (LTTE), 106–7
   suicide bomber, 107
Liberation War of 1971, 114, 118
Limaye, Madhu, 18, 39
Line of Actual Control, 97
Line of Control (LoC), 87
Lodha, R.M., 69
Lok Bhavan, 12–13

making of, 12–14
Lok Janshakti Party, 19
Lokpal Bill, 9
Lutyens, Sir Edwin, 179

Mahalanobis model, 36
Mahalanobis, P.C., 36
Mahendra, King, 100
Make in India, 37
Maldives, 110. *See also* Foreign policy
Malik, Sakshi, 37
Mandate Theory, 59
Marrakesh Declaration (1994), 173
Mauritius, taxation and, 121–23
   bilateral agreements, 122
   Double Taxation Avoidance Treaty (DTAA), 121
Mayawati, 20–21
   close links with, 20
   personal affinity for, 21
McMahon Line, 139
Mehta, Sir Pherozeshah, 8
Memon, Yakub, 76–81
Memorandum of Cooperation in the Road Transportation sector, 127
Menon, Shivshankar, 108
Mercy petition, 72–82
   Afzal Guru's case, 76, 80–81
   Ajmal Kasab's case, 75, 78, 80
   Bara massacre, 79–80
   broad outlines for dealing with mercy petitions, 74
   disposal of, 73, 82
   factors played, 74
   government favours a mercy petition, 79
   humane aspect, 72
   rarest of rare category case, 74
   recommendations of the government, 78
   rejected 30 mercy pleas, 73
   unanimous verdicts, 74
   Yakub Memon's case, 76–78, 80–81
Military or dictatorial rule, 63
Minh, Ho Chi, 125
Misra, Nripendra, 58
Modi Bangladesh visit (2015), 116
Modi, Narendra, 8–9, 12, 17–18, 23–24, 35, 39, 84–85, 94, 96, 104, 109–10, 114, 116–17, 119, 131, 136, 141, 150–51, 153, 155–57, 164, 168, 172–73, 175
   autocratic style of governance, 9
   conclusive mandate, 17
   cordial relations with, 24, 175
   decisive mandate, 24, 175
   detailed electioneering schedule, 17
   failed in its primary responsibility to, 8
   in-depth discussions Benjamin Netanyah, 136
   led NDA government, 8, 163
   no experience in foreign affairs, 84
   no ideological foreign policy baggage, 85
   not discussed the issue of demonetization, 156
   PM through popular choice, 173
   stopover in Lahore, 85
   Swachh Bharat Abhiyan, 35
Moral authority of opposition, 5–7
   agenda of disruptions, 5
Motilal Nehru Committee Report, 47
Mountbatten, Lord, 179
Mudgal, Shubha, 178
Mughal Gardens, 164
Muhith, Abul Maal Abdul, 118
Mukherjee, Ajoy, 57
Musharraf, General Pervez, 89
Muslim League, 19, 90, 114

Najibullah, Mohammad, 111
NAM summit, 141
Namboodiripad, E.M.S., 53
Namibia, liberation of, 141
Nanavati, K.M., 80
Narayanan, K.R., 171
Nasheed, Mohamed, 110
Nasser, Gamal Abdel, 141
National Democratic Alliance (NDA), 5, 8, 18, 163. See also Bharatiya Janata Party (BJP)
National Institution for Transforming India. See NITI Aayog
National Judicial Appointment Commission (NJAC), 65–67, 70
National Panchayat in Nepal, 100
Nationalist Congress Party (NCP), 20, 172
'Need' and 'greed', difference between, 41
Nehru, Jawaharlal, 2, 9–10, 23, 26, 36, 38, 47, 53, 92, 100, 105, 137, 141, 149, 151, 167–70
   area of difference with Rajendra Prasad, 170
   conflict of opinion, 2
   dealing with Nepal, 168
   demise of, 26, 151, 167
   friendship with Zhou Enlai, 1511
   functioning style, 168
   legacy of, 38
   longest term as PM, 167
   made presence felt on the floor of the House, 9
   practice of debate, discussion and dissent flourished, 2
   refuge to Dalai Lama, 137
      work with two presidents and two governor generals, 169established the norms of

constitutional propriety, 170
Nepal
   2001 palace massacre, 101
   civil unrest and Maoist attacks, 101
   communist reprisal in, 21
   emergency declaration (2005), 102
   multiparty democracy in, 103
Nepal Democratic Party, 100
Nepal, Madhav Kumar, 101
Nepali National Congress, 100
Nilekani, Nandan, 161
9/11 terrorists attack, 92, 95
Nirbhaya rape-and-murder, 30
NITI Aayog, 35
Nkrumah, Kwame, 141
Non-Aligned Movement (NAM), 141
Non-Proliferation of Nuclear Weapons, or Non-Proliferation Treaty (NPT), 92
Nonviolence, power of, 41
Nordic diplomacy, 126–30
North Atlantic Treaty Organization, 127
North-West Frontier Province, 115
Norway, peace-loving country, 126
Nuclear Suppliers Group (NSG), 97
Nujoma, Sam, 141

Obama, Barack, 95, 144, 151–54
   personal gift from, 153–54
Official Development Assistance (ODA), 149
Oli, K.P.S., 101, 148
123 Agreement (civil nuclear cooperation agreement), 126, 132, 139
Operation Blue Star, 171
Out-of-thebox initiative, 84

Pakistan. See Indo-Pak relations

Pakistan-occupied Kashmir (PoK), 90, 98
Palestine Liberation Organization, 135
Parliament sessions
  budget Session, 3
  culture of meaningless disruptions, 1
  debates and discussions, 4
  disruption of proceedings, 4–5
  drop in the number of days, 4
  institutionalized disruptions, 3–5
  meaningless disruptions, 3
  monsoon session, 3
  Nehru's prime ministership, 2
  winter Session, 3
Parliamentary form of government, 100, 175
Parliamentary journey, 1
Parliamentary standing committees, 4, 162
  role played, 4
Partition of India, 45, 47, 86–87, 111
  Unfinished agenda of, 87
  blocked the road route to Afghanistan by Pakistan, 111
Paswan, Ram Vilas, 19
Patel, Ahmed, 13
Pathankot, terrorist attack on a military base, 88
Patil, Pratibha, 73, 171
Patil, Shivraj, 21
Paul, Omita, 139
Pawar, Sharad, 172
People's Liberation Army of China, 92
People's Republic of China (PRC), 95
Per capita industrialization, 32
Personal friendships, oppose the expressions of, 151
PL 480, 93
Planning Commission, 35–36, 130, 145, 173
  scrapping of, 36
  See also NITI Ayog
Political parties, transparency in the funding of, 10
Politics, criminalization of, 10
Populist anarchy, 16
Post-Emergency electoral defeat, 38
Prabhakaran, V., 106–7
  extradition of, 107
Pradhan Mantri Jan Dhan Yojana, 35
Pranab Mukherjee Public Library, 180
Prasad, Rajendra, 26, 147, 153, 170, 179
Premadasa, Ranasinghe, 107
Preparing for polls, 21–22
President Rule, 50, 52–55, 57–58
President speech, 27
  economic challenges (2012), 32
  first address to the nation, 31–32
  Independence Day (2016), 34
  preliminary discussions, 31
  rehearsals, 31
  Republic Day (2013), 30
  Republic Day (2015), 33
  studio-friendly dress, 31
Presidents, 169–73
  B.D. Jatti (vice president acting as president), 169–170
  Fakhruddin Ali Ahmed, 170
  Giani Zail Singh, 170
  Justice Mohammad Hidayatullah, 169
  K.R. Narayanan, 171
  Neelam Sanjiva Reddy, 170
  Rajendra Prasad, 169–70
  S. Radhakrishnan, 170
  V.V. Giri, 169–70
  Zakir Hussain, 170
Prevention of Terrorism Act, 76
Prime Ministers, 167–71
  Atal Bihari Vajpayee, 171

Chandra Shekhar, 167
Charan Singh, 167–68
H.D. Deve Gowda, 167
I.K. Gujral, 167–68
Indira Gandhi, 167–68, 170
Jawaharlal Nehru, 167
Lal Bahadur Shastri, 168
Manmohan Singh, 168, 171
Narendra Modi, 168
P.V. Narasimha Rao, 168
Rajiv Gandhi, 168
V.P. Singh, 168
Provincial dyarchy, abolition of, 46
Pul, Kalikho, 55
Putin, Vladimir, 131–35

Question Hour, 7–8
Qureshi, Shah Mehmood, 90

Radhakrishnan, S., 26–27, 33, 170
    last Republic Day address, 26–27
Rahman, Sheikh Mujibur, 120
Railway budget, merger with general Budget, 37
Rajagopalachari, C., 179
Rajapaksa, Mahinda, 108–9
Rajkhowa, J.P., 54
Ram temple, issue of construction, 19
Ramachandran, M.G., 106
Ramdev, Baba, 181
Ramgoolam, Navin, 121–22
Rao, Narasimha, P.V., 5, 15, 39, 83, 93, 107, 136, 168
    economic reforms by, 93
    formed government in 1991 without any other party, 15–16
    issue of the extradition of Prabhakaran, 107
    short-lived government, 5
Rashtrapati Bhavan, 12–13, 17, 25–26, 43, 85, 120, 137, 147–48, 152, 156, 164–65, 177–82
    60 lakh people visited, 12
    adoption of Haryana's villages to make them model 'Smart Grams', 180
    alternative systems of medicine, 181
    cultural programmes, 178
    determination to connect with the common man, 179
    dinner for the visiting dignitaries, 85
    energy-efficient lighting systems, 180
    first-ever museum was inaugurated, 180
    in-residence programme, 180
    interest in the restoration of Rashtrapati Bhavan Library, 179
    meeting with Dalai Lama, 137
    meeting with various Congress leaders, 17
    open to ordinary citizens through online booking, 178
    publication of a multi-volume project, 181
    Rainwater harvesting techniques for residential quarters, 180
    renovation of guest wing, 120, 148
    'Samagam' for senior citizens, 180
    'Sanskriti' programme, 180
    solar water-heating arrangements, 180
    'Sparsh' for specially abled, 180
    tenure of Dr S. Radhakrishnan, 26
    waste-water recycling, 180
    welfare measures to improve the lives of residents of, 180
    yoga camp by Baba Ramdev, 181
    See also Lok Bhavan
Rashtriya Janata Dal, 20
Rashtriya Svayamsevak Sangh (RSS),

19
Rau, B.N., 49
Rawat, Harish, 57–58
Rebia, Nabam, 54
Reddy, Neelam Sanjiva, 170
Rehana, Sheikh, 117, 120
Religious fundamentalism, rise of, 88
Religious fundamentalists, 88
Republic Day, 16, 22, 25–26, 28, 30, 33, 95, 143, 145, 148, 150–52
　addresses, 28
　chief guest
　　Barack Obama (2015), 151–52
　　King of Bhutan, His Majesty Jigme Khesar Namgyel Wangchuck (2013), 145
　　Sinzo Abe (Japanese PM) (2014), 148
　choice of a chief guest, 144
Reserve Bank of India (RBI), 158
Right of Line: The President's Bodyguard, 181
Right to Fair Compensation and Transparency in Land Acquisition, Rehabilitation and Resettlement Act, 35
Rivlin, Reuven, 135
Rohingya crisis, 121
Rumsfeld, Donald, 93
Rupee-Rouble agreement, 134

S&T Cooperation Agreement, 127
S.R. Bommai cases, 58
SAARC, 24, 106, 111–13
Sabka saath, sabka vikas, 35. See also Modi, Narendra
Sairam, Aruna, 178
Salve, N.K.P., 7
Samajwadi Party, 19, 21
Sangma, P.A., 172

Saran, Shyam, 102–3
Sastri, V.S. Srinivasa, 8
Sathasivam, P., 69
Satyamurthy, S., 8
Saud, Abdul Aziz Ibn (Saudi King), 147
Second World War, 46
Sectarian conflicts, 33
Sen, Shekhar, 178
Sen, Surya, 120
Senanayake, Don Stephen, 105
Senanayake, Dudley, 105
Sepoy Mutiny (1857 revolt), 45
Shah Commission, 170
Shah, CJI J.C., 170
Shanghai Cooperation Organization, 99
Shangri-La Dialogue, 96
Sharif, Nawaz, 84–85, 89
Sharma, S.D., 22, 56
Shastri, Lal Bahadur, 26, 87, 167–68
Shinde, Sushil Kumar, 21, 74, 77
Shriram Bharatiya Kala Kendra, 178
Sindhu, P.V., 37
Singh, Beant, 52
Singh, C.P.N., 99
Singh, Charan, 6, 25, 167–68
Singh, Darbara, 52
Singh, Giani Zail, 52, 58, 170
Singh, Manmohan, 6, 9, 13, 19–20, 30, 39, 83, 85, 93, 102, 108, 116–17, 145–46, 148, 158, 168, 171–74
　appointed as finance minister, 93, 173
　Bangladesh visit, 116–17
　excellent sense of understanding, 174
　long working relationship with, 173
　made presence felt on the floor of the House, 9
　observed result of demonetization, 158

opposed the tendency disruptions, 6
preoccupied with saving the
  coalition, 9
prolonged absence from the House,
  20
tendered his resignation, 85
Singh, Rajnath, 23, 78
Singh, V.P., 19, 167–68
Singh, Zail, 171
Singye, King Jigme, 147
Sinha, Yashwant, 94, 122, 162
Sino-Indian relationship, 137–38
Sisodia, Manish, 13
Skill India, 37
'Smart Grams', 180
Solih, Ibrahim Mohamed, 110
South Asian Association for Regional
  Cooperation (SAARC), 24, 84, 106,
  111–13
South China Sea problem, 124
Sri Lanka, 105–10
  anti-terror measures, 107
  attack on Rajiv Gandhi by army
    man (1987), 107
  Chinese presence in the name of
    infrastructure development, 109
  cultural linkages through Buddhism,
    105
  economic cooperation, 105
  Indo-Sri Lanka Free Trade
    Agreement (1998), 106
  military assistance provided by India
    against LTTE, 106
  Modi's desire to improve the
    strained relations, 109
  relation influenced by Tamil politics
    in India, 106
  See also Foreign policy
Stability and instability, neutral
  between, 22

State business, commitment for, 30
State-of-the-art indirect taxation, 163
States Reorganisation Act of 1956,
  48–49
Subsidiary Alliance, doctrine of, 46
Swachh Bharat Abhiyan, 35
Swaraj, Sushma, 23

Tagore, Rabindranath, 120, 128–29,
  133
  advocacy for, 129
  relevance of, 128
Taliban, 91, 111
Tamil Eelam, 106
Tashkent Declaration, 87
Teesta water-sharing dispute, 116–18,
  120–21
Telangana, 21, 49
Terrorist and Disruptive Activities
  (Prevention) Act (2007), 77
Thakur, T.S., 69
Tito, Josip Broz, 141
Trinamool Congress, 20
Truman, Harry, 153
Trump, Donald, 95
Truth and non-violence, deployment
  of, 129
Tuki, Nabam, 54
Turkish Dervishes, 178
Turkmenistan-Afghanistan-Pakistan-
  India (TAPI) project, 133
26/11 Mumbai massacre, 75
Tyagi, Mahavir, 157

UN Security Council (UNSC), 93,
  95, 97
United Liberation Front of Asom
  (ULFA), 115
United Nations (UN), 81, 127, 135,
  168

United States, understanding with, 151–54
UPA-I, 19, 160
UPA-II, 19–20, 29
US–China relationship, 96

Vajpayee, Atal Bihari, 2, 9, 22, 39, 90, 115, 160, 168, 171
    differences of opinion between President K.R. Narayanan, 171
    first BJP leader to become PM for six years, 168
    formed a committee to review the GST plan, 160
    invited to form the government after a hung House in 1996, 22
    made presence felt on the floor of the House, 9
Value-added tax (VAT), 160, 165
Verma, Richard, 154
Viswanathan, T.K., 22
Voluntary Disclosure of Income and Wealth Ordinance, 1975, 157
Voting preference, 10

Wangchuck, Jigme Khesar Namgyel, 145, 147
Warsi brothers, 178
Wellesley, Governor General Lord, 46
Women empowerment—*nari shakti*, 37
Women's Reservation Bill, 10
World Trade Organization (WTO), 98, 173

Yadav, Mulayam Singh, close links with, 20

Yeltsin, Boris, 131

Zardari, Asif Ali, 75
Zedong, Mao, 92
Zerang-Delaram highway, 112
Zia, Khaleda, 118
Zia-ul-Haq, 87, 89